A Manager's Guide t

IT Law

The British Computer Society

The British Computer Society is the leading professional body for the IT industry. With members in over 100 countries, the BCS is the professional and learned Society in the field of computers and information systems.

The BCS is responsible for setting standards for the IT profession. It is also leading the change in public perception and appreciation of the economic and social importance of professionally managed IT projects and programmes. In this capacity, the Society advises, informs and persuades industry and government on successful IT implementation.

IT is affecting every part of our lives and that is why the BCS is determined to promote IT as *the* profession of the 21st century.

Joining the BCS

BCS qualifications, products and services are designed with your career plans in mind. We not only provide essential recognition through professional qualifications but also offer many other useful benefits to our members at every level.

Membership of the BCS demonstrates your commitment to professional development. It helps to set you apart from other IT practitioners and provides industry recognition of your skills and experience. Employers and customers increasingly require proof of professional qualifications and competence. Professional membership confirms your competence and integrity and sets an independent standard that people can trust. See www.bcs.org/membership for more information.

BCS Law Specialist Group

The Group keeps members informed of developments in computer law and holds meetings addressed by experts on computer contracts, Internet law, business to business communications, data protection, IT contracts, service level agreements, intellectual property in software and hardware, the use of computers in support of litigation, the arbitration of computer disputes and expert support in computer disputes. See www.bcs.org/groups for more information.

Further Information

Further information about the British Computer Society can be obtained from: The British Computer Society, 1 Sanford Street, Swindon, Wiltshire, SN1 1HJ. Telephone: +44 (0)1793 417424
Email: bcs@hq.bcs.org.uk
Web: www.bcs.org
Further information about the BCS Law Specialist Group can be obtained from: Jeremy Holt (Secretary)
Email: jeremyh@clarkholt.com

A Manager's Guide to
IT Law

EDITED BY

Jeremy Holt and Jeremy Newton

THE BRITISH COMPUTER SOCIETY

© 2004 The British Computer Society

The British Computer Society,
1 Sanford Street,
Swindon, Wiltshire SN1 1HJ,
UK
www.bcs.org

ISBN 1-902505-55-7

British Cataloguing in Publication Data.

A CIP catalogue record for this book is available at the British Library.

All trademarks, registered names etc. are acknowledged in this publication to be the property of their respective owners.

Disclaimer:

Although every care has been taken by the authors and The British Computer Society in the preparation of the publication, no warranty is given by the authors or The British Computer Society as to the accuracy or completeness of the information contained within it and neither the authors nor The British Computer Society shall be responsible or liable for any loss or damage whatsoever arising by virtue of such information or any instructions or advice contained within this publication or by any of the aforementioned.

Typeset and printed by J. W. Arrowsmith Ltd., Bristol

Contents

Contributors ix

Foreword   RICHARD CHRISTOU xi

Acknowledgements xii

Abbreviations xiii

Glossary xiv

Useful Organizations xviii

Preface   JEREMY HOLT xix

1 IT Contracts   JEREMY HOLT 1

Introduction 1

Parts of a contract 1

Who are you going to call? 2

Checking out the supplier 2

Letter of intent 3

The supplier's terms 3

What contracts are there likely to be? 3

Appendix: Main points of an IT contract 12

2 Systems Procurement Contracts   JEREMY NEWTON 14

The negotiation process 14

Contract mechanics 16

Commercial highlights 19

Problem management 21

Conclusion 26

Appendix: The 'reasonableness' test in practice 26

3 Implementing New Systems   JEAN MORGAN 29

Introduction 29

Setting realistic expectations 30

Specifying the correct requirement 31

Scoping the project   32

Planning   33

Realizing benefits   35

IT in mergers and acquisitions   35

IT due diligence   35

Conclusions   37

References   37

4 Avoiding Employment Problems   JEREMY HOLT   38

Introduction   38

Computer and email usage policies   38

Avoiding health and safety claims   43

Appendix: Specimen policy for computer and email use   46

5 Instructing an IT Consultant   JEAN MORGAN   50

Introduction   50

So you think you need a consultant?   50

Finding a consultant   51

Selecting the right consultant   54

Pricing structures   55

Assessing skills and knowledge   56

Getting value from the consultant   56

When all else fails   57

Appendix: Template for a terms of reference document   58

References   60

6 Intellectual Property Law for Computer Users   JENNIFER PIERCE   61

Introduction   61

Hardware and intellectual property rights   62

Software and intellectual property rights   63

Databases and intellectual property rights   65

Websites and intellectual property rights   66

Domain names and intellectual property rights   67

The internet and trade marks   69

The internet and copyright   70

Appendix: A basic guide to intellectual property and related rights 70

7 Source Code Escrow   GRAHAM WOOD   76

Introduction   76

The importance of escrow for software users 76

When do you need escrow? 77

Technical considerations 79

Verification 80

What should be lodged? 80

The agreements 81

User's duties 82

Choosing an escrow agent 82

Advantages of escrow for software owners 83

Conclusion 83

8 Outsourcing JEREMY NEWTON 85

Introduction 85

Defining the services 86

Design risk 87

Service level agreement 87

Pricing and payment mechanisms 89

The outsourcing life cycle 91

Other relevant issues 94

9 Data Protection ANDREW KATZ 95

Introduction 95

What data are covered 96

Sensitive personal data 97

Who needs to notify? 98

How to notify 99

Data protection principles 101

Rights of data subjects 101

Exemptions 110

Penalties and enforcement 111

References 111

10 Doing Business Electronically JEREMY NEWTON 112

Introduction 112

Prior authorization 113

Information to be provided to clients 114

Forming contracts electronically 116

Performance and cancellation 118

	Jurisdiction	119
	Marketing communications	120
	Consequences of non-compliance	121
	VAT issues	122
	Other considerations	123
	Appendix: Consolidated information requirements	124
11	Setting up Joint Ventures ANDREW KATZ	125
	Introduction	125
	Joint ventures and IT projects	125
	Establishing a joint venture	126
	Structure of a joint venture	129
	The operating agreement	135
	Competition law	135
	Appendix: Checklist for a joint venture operating agreement	137
12	Resolving Disputes SARA ELLACOTT	139
	Introduction	139
	Dispute resolution methods	139
	Conclusion	150
	Index	151

Contributors

Sara Ellacott is a partner in Nabarro Nathanson's Technology Media and Telecommunications Sector Group (www.nabarro.com). Sara handles a mixture of IT, IP and ecommerce related dispute work, advising on issues arising out of IT projects, interpreting contracts, copyright, trade marks, domain names, confidential information and email usage policies. She has experience in a wide range of dispute resolution procedures including negotiated settlements, High Court litigation, arbitration and mediation. She speaks regularly on issues relating to risk and dispute management.

Jeremy Holt is the head of the Computer Law Group of Clark Holt Commercial Solicitors (www.clarkholt.com). He has specialized in IT and ecommerce law for over 15 years. In 2003, Jeremy helped set up, in Swindon, the first museum in the country dedicated to the history of computing. He is the Secretary of the Law Specialist Group of the British Computer Society. Jeremy writes and lectures extensively on IT law and contracts.

Andrew Katz is a partner at Moorcrofts Corporate Law, a niche corporate and commercial legal practice based in Marlow, Bucks, and specializes in technology, media and telecomms work. He trained in London and moved to a large Midlands firm where he became their youngest-ever partner. Andrew was previously a computer consultant and was one of the first people to advise public bodies on data storage and retrieval using optical (CD-ROM) technology, and he became an acredited developer for Steve Jobs's NEXT computer system. He is currently interested in the legal challenges of open source software and peer-to-peer networking. He has been a member of the board and council of the Telecommunications Industry Association.

Jean Morgan (www.wilhen.co.uk) is an independent IT management consultant and has been listed on the BCS Consultants' Register since its inception. She has led a number of high-profile projects in the financial and defence sectors, as project or programme manager. Jean also works in IT due diligence and as an Expert Witness on IT procurement and forensic computing issues.

Jeremy Newton is a partner in the Technology Group at Nabarro Nathanson (www.nabarro.com), which he joined in September 2001 after a period as Assistant General Counsel with Sun Microsystems. He has specialized in IT and ecommerce law for over 10 years and is noted as a 'leader in the field' in Chambers' *Guide to the Legal Profession* and the Euromoney *Guide to the World's Leading IT Advisers*. Jeremy is on the editorial advisory board of *Electronic Business Law* magazine and he writes and lectures extensively on IT law and contracts.

Jennifer Pierce, a partner in the law firm Charles Russell (www.cr-law.co.uk), advises both customers and suppliers in the UK and overseas in respect of legal issues relating to software, equipment, peripherals, and other associated technology as well as internet and data usage. Her clients range from household names to private individuals. Jennifer writes and lectures widely on intellectual property and information technology. She is the joint editor and a major contributor to *Working with Technology: Law and Practice* published by Sweet & Maxwell, a visiting lecturer of the Queen Mary Intellectual Property Research Institute, and has appeared as an expert on BBC current affairs programmes.

Graham Wood is an attorney at Appleby Spurling & Kempe of Hamilton, Bermuda (www.ask.bm) and is also a consultant to Cobbetts of Manchester, England. He spent four years with the National Computing Centre in Manchester where he was a lawyer in the Escrow Department. Graham is currently a member of the Working Committee revising Bermuda's Intellectual Property legislation. He is also a member of the Computer Law Association, the American Bar Association and the International Trade Mark Association. He speaks on IT and IP law internationally and has written a number of articles on the subjects.

Foreword

Since the 1940s, when the computer first made its appearance, there has been a tremendous change in both the power and the extent of IT technology. It has evolved from mainframes through personal computers with packaged applications and client–server architectures, to the explosion of networking in the 1990s which led to the internet. Currently the IT industry is facing the challenges of mobile computing. Since each stage was incremental, the current state of IT technology is complex and requires considerable understanding.

Nowhere is this more important than the area of the law which applies to IT technology. The changes in technology have driven changes in IT law and contracting. We have come from what was a relatively scarce technology, supplied by experts to experts and used by experts, to a ubiquitous technology supplied through many different channels and used by everybody in their everyday life at home and at work. In terms of procurement, we have moved from the very close links between a few IT vendors and a few large IT departments to a situation where this technology is procured and supplied in many ways by many different purchasers. Given these changes, it is important that the people who purchase and use IT technology in the current environment are aware of the basic outline of the law which applies to computers and its implications for the businesses that they run or are engaged in advising.

This book sets out to provide executives with a basic framework of understanding across all of the main topic areas. It requires no special knowledge of the law but is designed to point out to people without legal qualifications the best practice, opportunities and pitfalls when dealing with the acquisition and use of the computer technology they require in order to stay competitive in their businesses.

Thus the main purpose of this book is to alert business people to the situations and circumstances in which they need to consult lawyers, not to create legal experts. In my experience, many problems in IT contracting could have been avoided if the people involved had had earlier input from their legal advisers. This requires not only that legal advisers be proactive but also that business people understand about using their services and be willing to do so.

The book also aims to help purchasers of IT to become more informed in their dealings with IT suppliers. I am delighted with this approach, since the best customers to work with are those who know what they want and are able to deal intelligently with their suppliers both during contract negotiations and delivery of their contract.

This book should help towards both of these desirable ends and I am more than happy to recommend it to business readers.

Richard Christou
Chief Executive
Fujitsu Services

Acknowledgements

The authors wish to thank the following people for their valued support in producing this book:

Martin Bazen	Christopher Bromfield
Charles Caplin	Carmel Haynes
Dawn Holt	Isabelle Katz
Lucy Katz	Oscar Katz
Jo Kitney	Claire Lane
Diane Leonard	Antonia Newell
Melanie Newton	Adrian Phillips
Susan Singleton	Frank Taylor
Shirine Tiwari	

Abbreviations

ASP	Application service provider
BCS	British Computer Society
BPO	Business process outsourcing
CPR	Civil procedural rules
CRM	Customer relationship management
DMA	Direct Marketing Association
DR	Dispute resolution
DSDM	Dynamic systems development method
DSE	Display screen equipment
DTI	Department of Trade and Industry
EEA	European Economic Area
EEIG	European Economic Interest Grouping
EMU	Economic and Monetary Union
ERP	Enterprise resource planning
HSE	Health and Safety Executive
IMC	Institute of Management Consultants
IPR	Intellectual property right
IT	Information technology
JV	Joint venture
LLP	Limited liability partnership
MCA	Management Consultants Association
MIT	Massachusetts Institute of Technology
MPS	Mailing Preference Service
NDA	Non-disclosure agreement
OEM	Original equipment manufacturer
OFT	Office of Fair Trading
PRINCE	Projects in a controlled environment
RAD	Rapid application development
RSI	Repetitive strain injury
SI	System integrator
SLA	Service level agreement
SSADM	Structured Systems Analysis and Design Method
TCC	Technology and Construction Court
TOR	Terms of reference
TUPE	Transfer of Undertakings (Protection of Employment) Regulations
VAT	Value added tax

Glossary

Acceptance Testing The running of a set of programs, under designated conditions, on a computer before the acceptance of the system by the customer.

Alternative Dispute Resolution (ADR) A method of settling disputes without resorting to the legal courts. Examples include mediation and expert determination.

Application Service Provider (ASP) A business that rents out the use of software running on its own servers to remote customers using a web-based connection to access the service.

Business Process Outsourcing (BPO) The sub-contracting by a business of some or all non-core business activities allowing it to concentrate on its principal activities.

Change Control The process for changing customer requirements during a project.

Civil Procedure Rules (CPR) The rules of practice and procedure that apply to the conduct of civil litigation in England and Wales.

Claimant The person who brings a legal action before the courts in England and Wales (formerly called the plaintiff).

Competition Law The law relating to the abuse of market power by buyers or sellers such as price fixing, cartel and the abuse of monopolies (also called anti-trust law).

Cookie A tag sent by a server to an internet user which is sent back to the server each time the internet user accesses that server.

Copyright A right for the creator of an original literary, dramatic or musical work to prevent the copying of such work. The right lasts for the life of the creator plus 70 years. No registration is required in the United Kingdom.

Customer Relationship Management (CRM) An integrated information system that is used to run the pre-sales and post-sales activities of a business.

Database Right A right under European law for the creator of a database to prevent the copying of such a database for 15 years. No registration is required.

Data Controller A person who holds information about a living individual either on a computer or in structured manual records.

Data Subject A living individual about whom another holds information on a computer or in structured manual records.

Decompiler A program that generates high level source code from machine code.

Defendant The person against whom a legal action is brought in the courts in England and Wales.

Design Right A right to prevent the copying of the external appearance of a manufactured article. Such protection can last for 25 years from the time of registration.

Display Screen Equipment (DSE) Computer monitors and any other screens that display text, numbers or graphics.

Dispute Resolution (DR) The settling of an argument between two parties.

Distance Selling A sale where the buyer and seller do not meet face to face e.g. sales via the internet, sales catalogue, fax or telephone.

Domain Name The address of an internet site, including a host name, sub-domain and domain, separated by dots (e.g. www.bcs.org.uk).

Due Diligence The process of investigation into a business or intellectual property rights before their purchase or entry into a contract relating to them.

Economic and Monetary Union (EMU) The consolidation of European currencies into the monetary unit of the euro which began in 1999.

Enterprise Resource Planning (ERP) A software system designed to support and automate the business processes of medium and large businesses.

Escrow The process of an independent third party holding something in readiness for a possible event. One example is an escrow agent holding the source code of software which would be released to a customer if the supplier became insolvent.

European Economic Area (EEA) The countries of the member states of the European Union, Iceland, Liechtenstein and Norway.

Facilities Management The management of a user's computer installation by an outside organization.

Force Majeure A supervening event such as a general strike or outbreak of war that a contract provides will validly prevent one party to the contract from carrying out its obligations to the other party.

Framing A method of including one page from the web within what appears to be another page.

Information Commissioner A government official in the United Kingdom who holds a register of data controllers and enforces data protection legislation (formerly known as the Data Protection Registrar).

Information Technology (IT) The application to information processing of current technologies from computing, telecommunications and micro-electronics.

Intellectual Property Right (IPR) Legal rights for the owners of inventions, designs and other materials to control their publication or use. Examples include patents, trade marks and copyright.

Interface Software that enables a program to work with the user, with another program or with the computer's hardware.

Joint Venture (JV) An arrangement between two (or more) businesses under which they work jointly for a common purpose.

Linking In a web page, the process of using a hypertext connection or highlighted piece of text to move the reader to another page.

Metatag A tag that identifies the contents of a web page (such as a key word for search engines).

Moral Right The right of the author of a copyright literary work to be identified as its author and for the work not to be subjected to derogatory treatment.

Non-Disclosure Agreement (NDA) A contract between a customer and a service provider under which one (or both) will keep various matters confidential.

Object Code The list of machine code instructions produced by passing the source code of a computer program through a compiler or an assembler.

Original Equipment Manufacturer (OEM) A misleading term for a business which repackages material made by other businesses. Unlike a value added reseller, an OEM does not necessarily add anything except their name to a product.

Outsourcing The assignment of tasks, such as payroll and data entry, to independent contractors outside the business.

Passing Off The action of a business giving the impression that it is (or is linked to) another business. This may be by the use of a similar name or other marketing get-up or the appearance of a product.

Patent A right granted by the state to an inventor of a new invention that, in return for a full public disclosure of the invention, the inventor will have a monopoly over the exploitation of the invention for up to 20 years.

Personal Data Information about a living individual.

Rapid Application Development (RAD) A software design cycle intended to give faster development and better results.

Repetitive Strain Injury (RSI) Damage to the hands, arms, neck, back or eyes due to computer use.

Sensitive Personal Data Information about a living individual that relates to their race, political opinions, religious beliefs, trade union membership, physical or mental health, sexual life or criminal record.

Service Level Agreement (SLA) A contract between two organizations about the quality of service to be provided by one to the other.

Source Code A textual description of a computer program, written in a programming language.

Spam Email that is not requested by the recipient (the word is taken from a repetitive Monty Python song).

Specification In relation to software, a description of the operating environment and proposed features and functionality of a new program; in relation to computer hardware, information about its capabilities and features.

Structured Systems Analysis and Design Method (SSADM) A technology that is widely used for the analysis and design of IT systems.

Subject Access Request The right under data protection legislation in the United Kingdom for an individual to ask a data controller what information it holds about that individual.

Systems Integration (SI) The combining of different programs or components into a functional system.

Systems Procurement The choice and purchase of a new computer system.

Technology and Construction Court (TCC) A division of the High Court of England and Wales that deals with technically complex legal claims.

Trade Mark A graphic sign which is capable of distinguishing the goods or services of one organization from another. A trade mark can last indefinitely (including where it has been registered).

Transfer of Undertaking (Protection of Employment) Regulations (TUPE) Legislation in the United Kingdom that preserves the employment rights of individuals upon the sale of the business in which they work.

Value Added Tax A sales tax applied in the United Kingdom.

Verification The process of confirming that a result is correct or that a procedure has been performed.

Useful Organizations

BCS Professional advice register   Web: www.bcs.org
BCS Worklink service   Web: www.worklink.org.uk
British Standards Institute   Web: www.bsi.org.uk
Department of Trade and Industry   Web: www.dti.gov.uk
Direct Marketing Association   Web: www.dma.org.uk
DSI Technology Escrow Services, 21 Terry Avenue, Suite 100, Burlington,
MA 01803, Telephone: (US) 781-273-5432, ext. 144, Fax: (US) 781-273-5633
    Web: www.dsiescrow.com, UK contact email: jgromyko@dsiescrow.com
Dynamic Systems Development Method Consortium
    Web: www.dsdm.org
Fax Preference Service   Web: www.mpsonline.org.uk
Health and Safety Executive, Information line: 08701 545500, Publications:
01787 881165
    Web: www.hse.gov.uk
Information Commissioner, Office of the Information Commissioner,
Wycliffe House, Water Lane, Wilmslow, Cheshire, SK9 5AF, Telephone:
01625 545700
    Web: www.informationcommissioner.gov.uk
    Email: mail@notification.demon.co.uk
Institute of Management Consultancy   Web: www.imc.co.uk
International Standards Organization   Web: www.iso.org
Law Society   Web: www.lawsoc.org.uk
Mailing Preference Service   Web: www.mpsonline.org.uk
Management Consultancies Association   Web: www.mca.org.uk
NCC Group, Manchester Technology Centre, Oxford Road, Manchester,
M1 7ED, Telephone: 0161 242 2200, Fax: 0161 242 2400
    Web: www.nccglobal.com
Office of Fair Trading   Web: www.oft.gov.uk/Business
Society for Computers and Law   Web: www.scl.org.uk
Stationery Office Ltd   Web: www.the-stationery-office.co.uk
Telephone Preference Service   Web: www.mpsonline.org.uk

Preface

This book is a practical guide for managers dealing with computer-related issues. The law in this area has changed so quickly that the contributors felt it should be summarized in a way that is easy to understand.

The book is not designed to be read from cover to cover. Readers can dip into the various self-contained chapters to find the answers that they seek. It provides practical advice on the appropriate steps that should be taken.

We trust that it will be a valuable guide to managers as well as being of interest to computer consultants, legal practitioners and students.

Jeremy Holt
www.clarkholt.com

1 IT Contracts

JEREMY HOLT

This chapter outlines the contents of a contract and lists the matters that should be covered by different types of contract. If you do not have time to read the rest of the chapter, the appendix lists the main points that you should consider.

INTRODUCTION

Pity the unfortunate manager. It has been bad enough trying to get the computer project organized. Now, possibly at the last moment, the contracts have arrived, some with print small enough to make the reader go blind. The manager suspects (rightly) that these contracts are one-sided in favour of the supplier, but knows that the project will only proceed if those contracts (or something similar) are signed. How does the manager work out what needs to be done and from whom advice can be obtained? This chapter provides a practical framework of help in this situation. If you are looking for an academic guide to computer contracts, you must look elsewhere.

PARTS OF A CONTRACT

The first point to consider is the form that contracts normally take. At its simplest a contract consists of:

i)   the date on which the contract was entered into;

ii) the names and addresses of those entering into the contract;

iii) a short description of what the contract is about (generally entitled 'Background', 'Recitals' or even, regrettably, 'Whereas');

iv) definitions of terms used in the contract;

v)   what the supplier is going to do for you;

vi) what you must do for the supplier;

vii) what you must pay the supplier.

Do not forget we are engaged in contract first aid here. If all else fails, concentrate on points (v) and (vii) i.e. what the supplier is going to do for you and what you are expected to pay.

Standard terms that are not specific to this individual contract (what lawyers call 'boilerplate') are generally grouped together at the end of the contract. A list of the more important boilerplate clauses is shown in the box.

IMPORTANT BOILERPLATE TERMS

Force Majeure – this says that neither party shall be liable for any failure to perform the contract because of circumstances beyond its control such as an Act of God, fire, flood, etc. This is likely to be invoked by the supplier more than the client. Because this clause effectively absolves the supplier from responsibility, the circumstances in which it can be invoked should be checked carefully so that they are no wider than is reasonable.

Entire Agreement – this says that the entire agreement between the parties is set out in the written contract and so no other previous representations by the supplier may be relied upon by the client. This is not an unreasonable principle but the client must make sure that the contract deals with all the important points.

Governing law and jurisdiction – ideally this should be English law enforced in the English courts. An alternative is to agree arbitration but as this happens behind closed doors then the supplier may worry less about bad publicity. It is sensible to agree an alternative dispute resolution procedure (such as mediation) which must be carried out before any dispute is referred to the courts or to arbitration.

WHO ARE YOU GOING TO CALL?

You are not going to be able to do all this on your own. You are going to need professional advice. Computer law is a specialist area (it did not exist 20 years ago) and the correct advice from a lawyer experienced in this field can save a great deal of trouble later. The function of a good lawyer is to assess risk, help the client to understand the level of risk and then reduce it.

There are two directories of lawyers that you might like to consult: Chambers' *Guide to the Legal Profession* and *The Legal 500*. New versions are published each year and each has sections on lawyers who specialize in computer law (sometimes called 'information technology law'). These two books can generally be found in the reference section of a public library. Alternatively, you can ring the Law Society or the Society for Computers and Law for suggestions of lawyers who work in this field and who could help you.

CHECKING OUT THE SUPPLIER

It may seem like an obvious point but make sure that you know who you are dealing with. This will mean, at least, doing a company search. A credit check would do no harm. As the Army maxim has it 'time spent on reconnaissance is seldom wasted'. If you discover that the supplier company was set up last year and has an issued capital of £2 you may like to consider asking for a guarantee of the contract from a more substantial body. Business is not all about making rational decisions. Do you get good vibes from the supplier? On small things, do they do what they say that they will do? If, for whatever reason, you do not trust them, do not go ahead with the contract under any circumstances as this will only lead to worry and tears later.

LETTER OF INTENT

As the supplier may need to start work on your project before contracts are signed and, because the negotiation and agreement of the contract terms may take a little while, the supplier may ask for a letter of intent from you. Alternatively you may like to suggest one so that you are not pressurized into signing the contracts before you have gone through them properly. A letter of intent is no more than written confirmation from you of your intention to enter into a contract with the supplier. What is critical, however, is that the letter of intent from you to the supplier must contain a statement that the letter is not intended to be contractually binding. Otherwise you may unwittingly enter into a contract earlier than you intended.

Where there is a non-binding letter of intent such as this and the supplier, at your request and to save time, starts work on the project, it is reasonable for the supplier to ask to be paid for this initial work carried out regardless of whether the project proceeds or not. There are two important matters to agree. The first is the rate for the job (e.g. a daily rate – work normally starts under a letter of intent on a time and materials basis; the definitive contract may include a fixed price for a specified deliverable). The other is an overall cap on your liability to the supplier for this work. This obligation to pay the supplier should be contractually binding (unlike the rest of the letter of intent).

THE SUPPLIER'S TERMS

There is of course no obligation on you to accept that you will purchase a new computer system on the basis of the supplier's terms. You could propose your own terms entirely – this is certainly an approach taken by large organizations with extensive experience of computer contracts. However, it is generally better to use the supplier's contract terms (unless they are completely unreasonable) as a start and amend them to your satisfaction. It is a good idea to ask for the supplier's proposed terms at as early a stage as possible. Do not wait until you have told them that they have been awarded the contract.

WHAT CONTRACTS ARE THERE LIKELY TO BE?

Any computer system will require the purchase of hardware (the server, PCs, printers, etc.), software (the application software and the operating system software) and services (such as support and maintenance). When computers first came out 20 or 30 years ago the emphasis was very much on the hardware, which was comparatively unreliable. Nowadays the emphasis is much more on the software and services. It is normal to decide upon the software first and then to choose the appropriate hardware.

If the contract relates to the procurement of a new system, the reader is referred to Chapter 2. The rest of this chapter deals with the purchase or licence of individual services or components.

Contracts for consultancy services

Long before the order for a new system is placed, the client may enter into a consultancy contract, perhaps relating to a feasibility study, analysing requirements, recommending a system to meet those requirements, helping select the appropriate suppliers, or assisting with preparation of an invitation to tender.

A large part of the work carried out in the computer industry is under a consultancy contract. The client may need help on a one-off basis or require skills which do not exist within the client's workforce. Hence there is a need for an outside consultant to carry out such work.

Sometimes the consultancy arrangement is dealt with by means of an exchange of letters; a formal consultancy agreement, however, is a better option for both parties. Some of the key issues to be addressed are set out below (see Chapter 5 for more details).

- Defining the deliverables. One of the most important issues that must be dealt with in such a contract is a detailed description of what the consultant is expected to do. If the description is loose or inexact, this can give rise to differences between what the client is expecting to receive and what the consultant is expecting to deliver – which can, predictably, lead to disputes. So defining the nature and quality of the deliverable is particularly important.

- Payment arrangements. The payment to the consultant by the client may be on a time and materials, fixed price or estimated maximum price basis. It is an aspect of consultancy that the amount of work required will be uncertain. The disadvantage of a fixed price payment mechanism (as with any other contract) is that the consultant will inevitably include a contingency element in the price quoted. If the consultancy can be broken down into a series of stages, payment against milestones will allow each party to gauge how the work is going.

- Copyright and confidentiality. Copyright will almost always be an issue. Broadly speaking, there is a simple choice as to how the parties deal with ownership of copyright in the consultant's work. Either the consultant can assign to the client all intellectual property rights in whatever is produced (provided that the consultant has been fully paid) or the consultant can grant a perpetual licence to the client to use such intellectual property rights for the purposes of the client's business (see Chapter 6 for more details).

- It goes almost without saying that the consultant should be obliged to keep confidential any information given by the client about its business. The problem is that once a consultant has carried out an assignment for one client in an industry, the consultant may be ideally placed to carry out assignments for other clients within that same industry. Sometimes, therefore, clients go further and stipulate in the contract that not only must their own information be kept confidential but the consultant must agree not to carry out projects for the client's competitors for perhaps a year after the work is completed.

- Insurance. In order to provide peace of mind to the client, the client may require the consultant to take out professional indemnity insurance. Despite the significant increases in insurance premiums in recent years, this is still relatively inexpensive. In practice, it is rare for claims to be made under such policies.

- Key personnel. The client will want to know the identity of the staff who the consultant will be using to carry out the work. It is normal for the client to be able to veto any staff members of whom they disapprove for whatever reason.

- The client will want to retain the right to terminate the consultancy contract if the consultant is guilty of serious misconduct or any other conduct likely to bring the client into disrepute.

Contracts for hardware purchase

Because computer hardware is so much more reliable than it used to be, contracts for the supply of hardware are not generally contentious.

A hardware purchase contract requires the following details:

- a detailed description of the hardware (this is likely to be in a schedule);
- a warranty about the quality of hardware (normally this warranty applies for a year after acceptance of the hardware by the client);
- delivery dates;
- price;
- acceptance testing;
- future maintenance;
- training.

Problems can arise if the hardware is not large enough for anticipated demand, and with the integration of hardware (such as servers and printers) which may have been supplied by different suppliers.

In many cases the cost of the hardware is not a large percentage of the total system cost. As profit margins on hardware are relatively low the software supplier may be relaxed about whether the client obtains the hardware from the software supplier or from a third-party supplier. It is always worth asking the software supplier to quote for supplying the hardware as they may have better bargaining power than you would have on your own.

At the end of the day, the two most important matters in a contract for hardware are to check that there is an exact description of what you are buying and that there is an obligation on the supplier to repair or replace it if it does not work properly.

Contracts for hardware maintenance

Hardware maintenance is more of a commodity than software maintenance and there are likely to be more alternative suppliers for the maintenance of hardware (and so prices are keener).

There are two different types of hardware maintenance – preventive maintenance and corrective maintenance. Preventive maintenance covers the regular testing of the hardware (e.g. once every six months) before any problem is reported. Corrective maintenance deals with faults as and when they arise, normally in response to a service call from the client. With corrective maintenance the key element is the response time – how quickly will the supplier start to respond to the problem once it is reported? This is generally within a fixed number of working hours. For example, an engineer may have to arrive at the site no more than eight working hours after the problem has been reported by the client. This does not mean that the engineer will solve the problem within eight hours – merely that a start will be made to try to solve it. Sometimes online diagnosis is used: the client's hardware is linked by telecommunications to the supplier who can solve the fault at a distance. (The impetus for online diagnosis came from the US where the distances were so great it was often not practicable to send an engineer in person.)

Payment for hardware maintenance is generally made in advance on a monthly or quarterly basis. The annual amount varies but can often be between 10% and 15% of the list price of the hardware. Other points that will normally be covered in a hardware maintenance contract include a right for the supplier to:

- make an additional charge for frivolous or unnecessary call outs;
- increase the charges from time to time, perhaps in accordance with a recognized index (such as the Retail Price Index);
- refuse to cover equipment which is more than five years old or which is past its reasonable working life.

The client will be under an obligation to:

- pay for corrections that are not caused by the equipment itself (e.g. faults arising from electrical fluctuations);

- notify the supplier of problems promptly after they arise (so that time does not make them worse);
- allow the supplier reasonable access to the equipment.

Contracts for software licences

At its simplest, any contract for software should allow you to use the software in the way that you envisaged without the risk that anyone can come along later and say either that you can not use it any more or that you have got to pay more money.

It follows, therefore, that one of the first checks that you should do is to confirm that the software supplier either owns the copyright in the software or has the right to license it to you. It is a feature of the computer industry that most software is licensed to end-users by organizations other than the actual owner (i.e. it is sublicensed, e.g. through a distributor). You should not put up with oblique answers to your demand for evidence that the supplier can license the software to you. They should be able to produce it immediately.

At this point you may wonder why a licence agreement is necessary at all. Why can the supplier not simply sell you the software? The supplier is not actually selling you ownership of the software (because they would like to continue to license it to other people). The licence is only a permit for you to use the software for your own purposes. This leads onto the next important point. You must check in the licence agreement to whom the software is licensed and for what purpose. Is the software to be licensed to your particular company or can it be used by the whole of your group (in which case the software supplier will want more money)? Alternatively, is the software to be restricted to a limited number of users and, if more than that number use it, then do you have to pay an additional licence fee? This is one of the oldest tricks in the software supplier's book. They allow the client to sign up for a very limited number of users and then the supplier makes a considerable profit from the additional users which will almost inevitably be required by the client later. The supplier, of course, responds that this simply reflects the extra use (and, as a result, commercial benefit) that the client is making of the software. It is also possible that at some time in the future the client may want to outsource its computer operations (see Chapter 8). Consequently, provision for the transfer of the licence from the client to an outsourcing company should be made in the original software licence agreement.

Contracts for software maintenance

No software of any complexity is ever free from errors. The older the system the more likely that it will need maintenance. Furthermore, if a system is installed in a rush (e.g. to meet a particular deadline) then it is likely not to have been tested properly and so require more attention after it has been installed. In some ways, future charges for maintenance are the icing on the cake for software developers. If they can generate sufficiently wide sales of the software then support fees can be guaranteed for years to come. It is important for managers to be aware of this as three-quarters of a budget for software may be for future software maintenance.

The client is well advised to check how wide the maintenance supplier's client base is (the wider the better) and to look at the offices from which the supplier will be providing the support (and how many people will be providing such support).

The maintenance contract will almost certainly be prepared by the supplier. Some of the most common provisions are discussed below.

- Charging arrangements. Sometimes the cost of the software licence is bundled with the first year's maintenance charges. One interesting point is from when the support charges should run. Some clients argue that they should start from the end of the warranty period for the software. However, it is now generally accepted that they should begin from acceptance of the system, as warranty and support are separate matters.

- Scope of maintenance services. Maintenance or support will normally cover the investigation by the supplier of errors in the system reported by the client as well as updated documentation and telephone or, more frequently nowadays, online advice. It will, in most cases, cover updates to the software (but not necessarily new versions of the software). The client may want to categorize different kinds of problems into those that could be critical for its business and those that are no more than an irritation and could be dealt with next time a new version of the software comes out. The supplier's response time will be different depending on the severity of the problem. The supplier will not normally commit to a fix within a particular period – only that they will start to fix it within a particular time.

- Exclusions from scope. The maintenance supplier will be keen to list in the contract what maintenance does *not* cover. Most of these exceptions are fair and reasonable. They generally include problems arising from changes to the software made by people other than the supplier, incorrect use of the software by the client or events beyond the control of the maintenance supplier such as hardware failure, fluctuation of electrical supplies or accidents.

Normally, the maintenance supplier will still seek to help the client where the exceptions apply (indeed there should be a contractual obligation to do so). However, the supplier may want to make an additional charge for such work and will not guarantee any particular recovery time. From the supplier's point of view it becomes difficult to manage support if the client base is using a number of different versions of the software. Consequently, the supplier normally restricts support to the latest two versions of the software and will refuse to support earlier versions.

- Charge increases. The client will want to ensure that the maintenance charges will not rocket up. One means of doing this is to tie the maintenance charges to a percentage of the list price of the software (e.g. 10–15%) but of course the supplier has control over the list price. Alternatively, any increase in maintenance charges can be tied to a recognized index. Clients sometimes suggest the Retail Price Index. However, suppliers (who know that increases in salaries are generally greater than increases in retail prices) prefer to tie them to an earnings index. There is some logic in this as the bulk of the supplier's expenses are salaries.

- Payment arrangements. Payment is almost invariably made in advance. In the past, it was for a year but now it is more commonly paid three months or a month in advance. This is so that if the supplier goes into liquidation the client will not have overpaid very much and the client can also swiftly withhold the payment of maintenance charges if there is a problem with the service provided.

- Termination. It is important for the client to look at the termination clauses of the contract offered by the supplier. The client will want to know how much notice they have to give to end the maintenance contract. This is often three or six months. It is a good idea for the client to ask the supplier to commit on its part to supply maintenance (if the client wants it) for the potential life of the software (e.g. five years).

Contracts for software development

Most software will need to be customized for the client by the supplier. However this is really only a tinkering with the main programs. In certain circumstances, it may be necessary for the client to commission new software because there is no existing software that meets the client's needs. Contracts for software development are complex and it is wise for the client to seek professional advice both about the specification for the software and the contract under which the software will be written. This is all the more important because software development projects have a reputation for taking longer, and for costing more, than originally forecast. Consequently background research by the client into the proposed supplier is particularly worthwhile.

Pricing for the project will be either fixed price or time and materials. Payments will normally be made conditional upon project milestones being reached.

The client will seek to ensure the quality of the software product delivered by the supplier by requiring acceptance tests of the software and a warranty from the supplier that the product will be in accordance with the agreed specification.

A thorny question is whether the client should own the copyright in the software program produced. At first glance, it might be thought that this should obviously belong to the client who has paid for it. However, all the client needs is to use the software; the client needs neither to own nor to develop it further. There is a benefit to the client in the supplier having an incentive to carry out further development of the software program and license it to other clients. The original client does not then pay the total cost of all the subsequent fixes and has the benefit of the faults reported by other users.

If the supplier becomes insolvent then the client needs access to the source code of the software in order to maintain it. For this reason the client should require the supplier to put a copy of such source code in escrow with an independent third party so that it is available if required (see Chapter 7).

The supplier will normally provide a warranty that defects in the software reported within a particular length of time after the start of its use will be rectified. This is frequently 90 days after acceptance of the software by the client.

Service level agreements

Service level agreements (SLAs) are critical to the computer industry but they are rarely fully understood. Under an SLA, a supplier undertakes to supply a service to a client at a particular level. Perhaps because so few lawyers have a reasonable working knowledge of the computer industry, SLAs are often drawn up by the participants without legal advice.

A service level agreement should cover:

- The service required (i.e. what the client wants and what the supplier is prepared to commit to supply);
- Quality standards (i.e. the standards or levels the supplier must achieve), such as host/terminal response times, batch processing times, 'uptime', or processor availability, by specifying what? when? how? and by whom?
- Deliverables (e.g. regular reports);
- The consequences of failing to meet service procedures or standards (e.g. compensation in the form of service credits);
- Procedures for the client to monitor performance of obligations by the supplier;
- Procedures for change control (i.e. changing part of the service that is being provided by the supplier under the agreement);
- Terms dealing with access to, and security of, the client's site and data;
- A procedure for disaster recovery (either upon a system failure or a catastrophe);
- The agreed frequency of meetings between the client and the supplier to review the supplier's performance of the agreement, properly minuted with subsequent action plans and awards of priority.

Ideally, an SLA should be a self-enforcing agreement within a continuing relationship. There should be no need for either side to litigate and changes required should be dealt with through a change control procedure. In some ways the process of creating the SLA is as valuable as the agreement itself. SLAs can be between different businesses or between different parts of the same organization (such as the IT department and its users). Facilities Management Agreements, Software Maintenance Agreements and Managed Data Network Agreements are all examples of SLAs. Alternatively, the SLA may be one aspect of a larger agreement for services, i.e. it may be the schedule that stipulates how well the services have to be provided and what happens if the supplier does not provide this.

What form should a service level agreement take?

At its weakest, an SLA may be a simple oral understanding, documented by an exchange of letters. The best form is a formal legal agreement with the technical procedures and specifications annexed as separate schedules.

What happens if the terms of a service level agreement are broken?

If the breach is fundamental, the party not in breach will be entitled to terminate the agreement and sue for the loss suffered as a result of the breach. In other circumstances there will be a system for measuring breach and apportioning cost. These systems range from an event-based system (i.e. if ... then ...) to a more sophisticated system of 'failure points' (i.e. if there are more than five examples of ... then ...). The functions of such compensation systems vary from simply drawing attention to a problem to compensation for loss. Compensation for loss is difficult to quantify and, if it is excessive, will be unenforceable by a court. In practice, the right to withhold payment is a valuable weapon. The end (or slowing down) of payments into the supplier's accounts department is likely to put pressure on the supplier.

Escalation clauses are undervalued and should be more widely used. These provide for a problem to be escalated up the various tiers of management on both sides if it cannot initially be resolved.

Even the best SLA does not last for ever and there must be a procedure for orderly termination and (if necessary) migration from the supplier's system to another system. The failure to include such clauses was a frequent weakness of early SLAs. Migration is critically important in relation to facilities management contracts and, as a rule of thumb, a year is generally allowed for this. The supplier should also be required to provide all reasonable assistance to the client with the migration to another system.

APPENDIX: MAIN POINTS OF AN IT CONTRACT

Read this on its own if you have not got enough time to read the rest of this chapter. But read it carefully.

i)   Make sure that you know exactly what you want and what is achievable because if you do not know, then you are not going to get the contract right. (Among the most common causes of computer project failure are unclear client requirements and unrealistic client expectations.)

ii) Make sure that all the prospective suppliers sign a confidentiality agreement with you. If you are going to give them a detailed functional specification of what you want and information about your business you do not want there to be any question of that confidential information being obtained by your competitors.

iii) Beware of falling into the trap of entering into a contract before you intend to. There are no legal formalities in this country about entering into a computer contract, so make sure that all pre-contract correspondence is headed 'subject to contract'. If you leave discussions about a written contract incomplete (e.g. lots of draft contracts sent between you and the supplier but nothing ever signed) then a court is likely to take the last undisputed draft as being the basis of the contract between you and the supplier.

iv) If a particular point is important to you make sure that you get it in writing from the supplier. It may well be that an aspect that is critical to you is not dealt with in the supplier's draft contract at all. If so, you must, for evidence's sake, get it in writing from the supplier. An ordinary letter from the supplier is sufficient provided that it is either referred to in the main contract or, possibly, included as a schedule or as an attachment. If the supplier drags its heels and, despite repeated requests from you, refuses to confirm a point in writing, you should write to the supplier saying that you are only entering into the main contract on the basis that this point is agreed. If the matter ever goes to court the production of your letter will be of great assistance to your case.

v)   Make sure that you get the supplier to agree to supply support and maintenance for the products purchased for a decent length of time, e.g. five years. You do not want the supplier cancelling support after a couple of years just when your new system is working well. Note that you do not have to commit to take the support and maintenance for five years – ideally your commitment should be on a year by year basis. It is just that the supplier agrees to make the support available to you for at least five years if you want it.

vi) Make sure that you order enough training. One of the most common reasons for the failure of a computer project is inadequate training. It is sadly all too common that, if there is an overspend in other areas, the amount budgeted for training is cut. As a rule of thumb, roughly 20% of a project's cost should be spent on training. If it is substantially less than that you should ask why.

vii) Make sure that the procedure for acceptance testing is known and agreed. If this has not been sorted out in the contract, how are you going to stop a bad system from being installed? In the past, the test data was generally supplied by the client; nowadays it is more acceptable for it to be provided by the supplier.

viii) Make sure that you can get access to the source code of the software programs supplied if the supplier either goes into liquidation or stops supporting the software. Ideally, this source code should be deposited with an independent third party (see Chapter 7) and kept updated by the supplier as each new version comes out.

ix) Finally, never forget that the contract is a delivery mechanism for ensuring that a project is completed in the right way at the right time by the right person and for the right price. No more, no less.

2 Systems Procurement Contracts

JEREMY NEWTON

Terms like 'computer contract' or 'systems procurement contract' cover a broad range of commercial transactions, from the purchase of a single CD-ROM from a high street retailer through to multimillion pound agreements for consultancy or outsourcing services. This chapter outlines the legal issues that need to be addressed in any contract of this type, using examples from actual case law to illustrate the kinds of dispute that commonly arise in relation to systems procurement, and discusses how the process of drafting and negotiating the agreement can be used to prevent some of the most common problems.

THE NEGOTIATION PROCESS

The function of a written contract is to record the terms governing the supply of goods and services. In the absence of a clear, express understanding between the parties, certain terms may be implied into the contract as a matter of law – for example, that products will be delivered within a 'reasonable' time and that they will be of 'satisfactory' quality. The main terms that can be implied into a contract as a matter of law are summarized in the box.

TERMS IMPLIED BY LAW

Certain terms may be implied into a contract as a matter of law: this means that the contract will include these provisions automatically, unless the parties expressly agree to exclude them. The main implied terms are summarized below.

Title: All contracts of sale include an implied term that the seller has the right to sell the goods in question (Sale of Goods Act 1979 s.12(1)). If the seller fails to transfer ownership (for example, because the goods are subject to the rights of some third party, such as a bank), then he will be in breach of this term and the buyer may reject the goods and recover the price, plus damages.

Quiet possession: This right is in effect a promise by the seller that no person will in the future acquire rights over the goods and enforce them against the buyer (Sale of Goods Act 1979 s.12(2)). If this should happen (for example, because the use of the product turns out to infringe some third-party intellectual property right), the buyer will be entitled to claim damages. In the worst case, where the third party exercises its rights in such a way as to prevent the buyer using the goods at all, the buyer's damages will be assessed as the cost of buying a replacement, in effect returning the original purchase price.

Correspondence with description: Goods must correspond with the description given by the seller (Sale of Goods Act 1979 s.13). This description can take many forms: a standard print-ed specification, an agreed user requirements specification, and claims made by the sales force or set out in the manufacturer's publicity material.

Quality and fitness for purpose: Goods must be of satisfactory quality and reasonably fit for their purpose (Sale of Goods Act 1979 s.14). 'Satisfactory quality' means that the goods meet the standard that a reasonable person would regard as satisfactory, taking account of any description of the goods, the price (if relevant) and all the other relevant circumstances.

Reasonable care and skill: The law also implies a term into contracts for services (such as consultancy, development or support), to the effect that the services will be provided with reasonable care and skill (Supply of Goods and Services Act 1982 s.13).

Apart from the above terms, which are implied as a matter of statute law, terms may also be implied from the facts and circumstances of the particular contract, if they are necessary to give 'business efficacy' to the contract.

However, given the vagueness of the implied terms and the unpredictability of their legal interpretation, any prudent buyer or seller of IT systems will want to ensure that the parties' intentions are recorded clearly and unam-biguously. The negotiation process that leads to the written contract should help ensure that the parties understand each other's expectations and com-mitments. Many IT projects fail precisely because the parties do not exercise sufficient care to ensure that their expectations match and often because of an uncritical acceptance of the supplier's standard terms of business.

Any well-drawn contract will have provisions relating to three broad cat-egories of expectation. The aim of the negotiation process is to ensure that no essential terms are missing from the final agreement, and this chapter will address each of the categories in turn:

- Contract mechanics: who delivers what, and when?

- Commercial highlights: what is the price, who owns the resulting intel-lectual property rights, what warranties are given in respect of the sys-tem?

- Problem management: what happens if the project goes wrong and what remedies are available?

BEWARE THE STANDARD CONTRACT

The dangers of agreeing unquestioningly to the standard supply terms (or for that matter, to a client's standard terms of procurement) are illustrated by the case of *Mackenzie Patten v. British Olivetti.*

A law firm bought an Olivetti computer system to run their accounts. They discussed their needs with the salesperson and signed up to Olivetti's standard terms. These dealt only with the system's technical performance: they did not address certain other important issues that had been discussed between the parties.

In the event, the system proved unsuitable for the firm's purposes: it was slow, difficult to use, and could not expand to cope with new business, but none of these matters was dealt with in the written contract. Even though a court found that Olivetti was bound by its salesperson's claims that the system would be suitable for the law firm's needs, the firm had by that stage expended significant time and money in the litigation and still had to find a replacement system.

Put another way, 'standard' forms are only suitable for entirely 'standard' transactions, and will often fail to address some essential point that the parties had in mind for their particular deal.

CONTRACT MECHANICS

Principal obligations

An IT contract need not be a complex document. It does not even need to be in writing, though this is clearly undesirable from the point of view of creating legal and contractual certainty as to each party's commitments to the other. In the simplest case, however, a written contract need say no more than this: that the supplier will provide a system X computer to the client; and that the client will pay £Y to the supplier.

That is the essence of the commercial relationship and there is nothing else (from the strict legal point of view) that requires to be said. However, if the aim of the contract process is to ensure that the project goes ahead smoothly and with the minimum scope for disagreement between the two sides, it is desirable for the contract to be considerably more specific in terms of what is being delivered, when and how.

Specification

A clear specification is the foundation stone of a successful systems supply contract. Although the law implies a term into a contract that the system will conform to its description and be of satisfactory quality, this is no substitute for ensuring that the supplier and the client agree and documenting, in as detailed a manner as possible, exactly what is to be provided and the performance and quality standards to be achieved.

Every system supply contract should, accordingly, include a detailed specification setting out:

- the required functionality (what the system is required to do);
- performance targets (how well it is supposed to do it);
- compatibility requirements for interfaces with other systems.

THE NEED FOR A FORMAL SYSTEM SPECIFICATION

The legal implications of not developing a proper specification are illustrated by the case of *Micron Computer Systems Ltd v. Wang (UK) Ltd.*

One of Micron's complaints against its supplier was that the Wang system did not provide 'transaction logging'. The judge observed that 'the acknowledged absence of a transaction logging facility is not in reality a fault in the system which was sold. Micron can only complain about its absence if Micron can establish a contractual term ... to the effect that the system included such a facility. In order to make good its case in transaction logging, Micron must therefore establish that they made known to Wang that they required such a facility'.

The judge found that Micron had not made its requirement for transaction logging clear to Wang and accordingly that part of Micron's case failed.

Timetable

The process of preparing the specification should enable the parties to assess the likely timescale for the project and to prepare a project plan setting out key deliverables (or 'milestones') and their expected dates. In almost all major systems implementations, staged payments will be triggered by the achievement of individual milestones. It is, accordingly, essential that these are identified with as much precision as possible and generally reflect the terminology of the contract.

The buyer will usually have in mind a timescale within which the system should be provided, although the sophistication of the timetable will vary according to the complexity of the project and how closely the payment arrangements are tied into the achievement of specific milestones.

Delivery

Although the law provides for an implied term that goods will be delivered 'within a reasonable time', delivery arrangements should always be dealt with expressly. From the point of view of contractual certainty, the ideal situation is for the contract to set out specific delivery dates, but it should also go on to deal with the 'mechanics' of delivery and installation. The contract should address:

- the date on which delivery is to be made;
- whether all the elements of the system are to be delivered at one time or whether it is to arrive in instalments;
- who has responsibility for installation and testing;
- the implications of late delivery or non-delivery (for example, an express provision permitting cancellation of the contract, with or without compensation to the buyer, if the goods are not delivered by some cut-off date).

Acceptance testing

Formal acceptance testing arrangements are a crucial aspect of any successful procurement. The system is required to meet the functions and performance targets set out in the specification, but until it is tested the parties can not determine whether those requirements have been met.

The nature of acceptance tests varies widely between projects. Where a major piece of development work is involved, the parties may negotiate and document detailed testing arrangements as part of the contract. At the other extreme, the acceptance procedure may simply be that if the buyer uses the system 'live' for, say, 30 days without rejecting it, then it is deemed to have been accepted.

From the point of view of creating contractual certainty, then, the acceptance procedure should:

- provide for an objective and measurable 'yardstick' as to the standards of performance and functionality to be demonstrated;
- address all those elements that are necessary to demonstrate, to the buyer's satisfaction, that the system meets its requirements;
- be clear as to the consequences of both the passing and failing of the acceptance test.

Acceptance will generally trigger payment of the whole or the final instalment of any lump sum charges, or the start of periodic charges, and following acceptance the buyer's remedies will be limited to a claim under the warranty provision.

In the event of failure of the acceptance tests, the contract will typically provide for a period during which the supplier may rectify problems and then retest; but further failure will signal the premature end of the contract, with the buyer able to return the hardware and software in exchange for a refund of any money paid.

Client obligations

The successful implementation of a complex IT system imposes responsibilities not just on the supplier, but also on the client. Although primary responsibility for providing a system rests with the supplier, the client may well have obligations in relation to providing information about his business, testing the software, providing employees to be trained and so on. These obligations need to be spelled out in the contract every bit as clearly as the supplier's commitments.

Change control

Client requirements may change frequently over the lifetime of a project. The parties need to agree a procedure for specifying and agreeing changes to the scope of work. The proper management and documentation of these changes will avoid disputes about what each party's obligations actually were.

The contract should include a formal 'change control' clause, setting out a mechanism whereby the client can request (and the supplier can recommend) changes to the specification, the project plan, or any other aspect of the deal. Any such change needs to be considered from the point of view of:

- technical feasibility;
- impact on the respective obligations of the supplier and client;
- cost implications;
- impact on the timetable.

As a general rule, no change should take effect unless it has been formally agreed and documented by both parties.

Termination

Provision has to be made for termination of the contract, setting out the circumstances in which the contract may be brought to an end and the consequences of that action. These provisions will vary according to the nature of the contract and the deliverables.

Apart from a general right to terminate the contract in the event of material breach or the insolvency of the other party, the following points should be considered:

- In relation to hardware procurement elements, the client may wish to cancel/terminate the contract before the delivery date. In that event the contract should set out the compensation payable to the supplier.
- Contracts for development services are typically terminable by the client if specific time-critical milestones are significantly overdue. Provision should be made for treatment of the developed software on termination, including delivery of all copies (and source code) and certification that no copies have been retained.
- Contracts for continuing services (consultancy, support and maintenance services, bureau services) should be terminable on notice. The length of the notice and the earliest dates on which it may be effective are matters of negotiation in each case.

COMMERCIAL HIGHLIGHTS

Pricing and payment

There are as many pricing and payment structures as there are types of IT deal, and there is little to be gained from making generalizations about pricing and payment terms. The one point worth making is that, where payments are tied into specific targets (such as system acceptance), the terminology and structure of the payment schedule should accurately reflect that of the timetable.

There are several payment-related mechanisms that are commonly used to ensure that both parties have incentives to perform their obligations:

- The client may wish to provide for payment by instalments as the various parts of the system are delivered, retaining a proportion of the price until the complete system has been tested. The retention of a significant proportion of the charges will give the buyer some assurance that the supplier will finish the job.

- In respect of periodic fees, specifically, the buyer will be concerned about the supplier's rights to increase the fee and may seek to limit rises by agreeing to, for example, only one increase a year or by tying increases to an appropriate index.

- It is common for hardware suppliers to retain title in the goods they supply as security for payment. This means that although the buyer gets possession of the goods, ownership remains with the seller until certain conditions (normally payment in full) are met. If the buyer fails to comply with the conditions, the seller can repossess the goods and sell them to recoup his losses.

Intellectual property rights (IPRs)

System supply contracts generally entail the transfer of technology and information from one party to another: for example, specifications, software, data and confidential business information. The lawful use of technology and information depends on compliance with the laws relating to copyright, confidentiality, database rights and other forms of intellectual property (see Chapter 6), so system supply contracts must deal comprehensively with IPR issues. There are two key IPR aspects to consider: ownership, and warranties and indemnities.

In relation to ownership, the contract should specify what IPRs are to be created or used, and precisely who owns them (including identifying the owners of any third party IPRs that are to be used or licensed). Copyright law contains a common trap for the unwary in relation to contracts for software development or consultancy work. The IPR in work undertaken by a contractor (as opposed to an employee) will normally vest in the supplier rather than the client. This means that an express, written assignment of copyright is needed if the aim is for the client to own these IPRs outright.

In relation to warranties, most system contracts will contain an assurance that the client's use of the system will not infringe third-party rights and an indemnity in respect of any claims that may arise against the client. The contract should set out any express warranties required by the client as to the supplier's ownership or entitlement in respect of the IPRs comprised in the system, together with a process for addressing any breach of those warranties.

In relation to the possible infringement of third-party IPRs, the client will typically impose a formal obligation for the supplier to deal with any such allegations – especially if the system is a critical part of the client's business and merely rejecting it and claiming back the purchase price would be insufficient. A typical IPR indemnity clause will provide:

- a right for the supplier to take over, litigate and/or settle any such action;
- a right for the supplier to modify the system so that it does not infringe the alleged right, provided that it still conforms with the specification;
- an indemnity given by the supplier against the client's losses in the event of a successful third-party claim.

Supplier warranties

The client will normally require the supplier to give certain other express assurances in respect of the system to be delivered. Ideally, the client will want to obtain a warranty that the system will comply with its specification and/or meet specified performance criteria.

Such warranties are often subject to time limits or other restrictions. It is not unusual for the supplier to seek to limit the warranty to, say, six months from acceptance: after that point, any defects are rectified under maintenance and support arrangements (paid for by the client) rather than under warranty.

PROBLEM MANAGEMENT

Contractual remedies

The parties must consider at the negotiation stage what happens if a contract does not go according to plan – for example, if the supplier fails to deliver a working system within the contracted time frames. Although damages and other remedies may be available as a matter of general law, it is preferable to spell out expressly the remedies that each party may have in particular situations.

One common mechanism for managing such disputes is to provide for payment of 'liquidated' damages for certain breaches. This involves setting out in advance the precise sum to be paid as compensation for certain breaches (e.g. late delivery at £X per day). Provided that sum is a genuine estimate of the likely losses and not a penalty to force the other party to perform, the clause will be enforceable.

If the breach in question persists for a specified time or reaches a specified level of severity, the innocent party may also want a right to terminate the contract outright.

Limitations and exclusions of liability

IT suppliers generally seek to restrict their potential exposure to actions resulting from breach of contract or defects in the system. This is treated by some as purely a 'legal' issue, but in fact is a major question of commercial risk assessment and allocation, and these provisions can be amongst the most hard-fought in any contract negotiation.

A typical standard exclusion clause may take the following form:

- the supplier does not exclude liability for death or personal injury caused by negligence;
- the supplier seeks to exclude liability altogether for certain kinds of loss, often termed 'special', 'indirect' or 'consequential'; and
- the supplier accepts a limited degree of liability for certain other classes of loss.

From the legal point of view, exclusion clauses need to be considered from two broad aspects. First, suppliers will often argue that they should have no liability for 'consequential loss', on the basis that the nature of IT products means that their uses (and so the potential losses resulting from failure) are not easily foreseeable at the time the contract is made and the potential exposure is in any case disproportionate to the contract value. Whether this is an acceptable commercial stance depends on the nature of the system and the extent of the client's dependence on it. However, the courts have exercised considerable ingenuity in manipulating and interpreting expressions like 'consequential loss' in ways that the parties may not originally have intended.

CONSEQUENTIAL LOSS: THE SEMANTIC LABYRINTH

Although they are commonly used in all sorts of commercial agreements, there is no legal consensus as to the meaning of the expressions 'special', 'indirect' and 'consequential' in the context of contractual claims, and there is often a resulting lack of certainty as to the precise effect of the intended exclusion.

The usual starting point for any discussion of consequential loss is the case of *Hadley v. Baxendale*. In that case, the court distinguished two classes of loss that could be recovered for breach of contract. These are:

- such [damages] as may fairly and reasonably be considered either as arising naturally, i.e. according to the usual course of things ... or such as may reasonably be supposed to have been in the contemplation of both parties at the time they made the contract as the probable result of the breach of it;
- if the parties were aware of 'special circumstances' at the time the contract was made, the damages 'which they would reasonably contemplate would be the amount of injury which would ordinarily flow from a breach under these special circumstances'.

That basic distinction has been reworked several times over the years, but the terminology that is widely used in IT contracts does not fit neatly into the *Hadley v. Baxendale* rules and in fact means different things to different people.

In fact, the most recent authoritative discussion of the meaning of 'consequential loss' is the case of *British Sugar Plc v. NEI Power Projects Ltd* , which really serves to illustrate the kind of philosophical confusion that can be caused by trying to use *Hadley v. Baxendale* terminology to describe contractual losses in terms like 'direct', 'indirect' or 'consequential'.

NEI supplied some defective power equipment, with a headline value of about £100000, to British Sugar. The sale contract expressly limited the seller's liability for 'consequential loss'. As a result of breakdowns, increased production costs and resulting loss of profits, British Sugar put in a claim of over £5 million. British Sugar argued for the narrowest construction of the term 'consequential loss', interpreting it to mean 'loss not resulting directly and naturally from breach of contract'; whereas NEI argued that the term meant 'all loss other than the normal loss which might be suffered as a result of the breach of contract, negligence or other breach of duty'. The court found for the claimant and approved earlier authorities that 'consequential damages' means the damages recoverable under the second limb of *Hadley v. Baxendale.*

By this analysis, where loss of profits or loss of business (commonly regarded as typical examples of 'consequential loss') arise naturally from the breach of contract, they should be recoverable by the user: a result that may surprise many IT suppliers.

Similar confusion applies in relation to other commonly-used terms. The term 'consequential' has at one point been defined simply to mean 'not direct'; but there is also judicial authority to suggest that 'direct loss' could include 'consequential loss' in certain circumstances.

Likewise, the term 'special damages' has no fewer than four possible meanings, including past (pecuniary) loss calculable as at the trial date – as opposed to all other items of unliquidated 'general damages'; and losses falling under the second rule in *Hadley v. Baxendale* – as opposed to 'general damages' being losses recoverable under the first rule.

Secondly, there is an extensive body of law relating to the enforceability of exclusion clauses generally: if the exclusion clause is found to be unreasonable or defective in some other way, then the party seeking to rely on the exclusion may nevertheless be exposed to a greater degree of legal and financial risk than it originally envisaged.

. The combined effect of the enforceability rules and the uncertainty about the meaning of commonly-used language is that clarity is of the utmost importance in the wording of exclusion clauses: it is not in anybody's interest for the effect of the exclusion to be uncertain and indeed it is surprising that businesses should continue routinely to use some of the terminology that regularly crops up.

Instead of debating abstract concepts like 'consequential loss', suppliers and clients alike should focus on the specific risks associated with the particular system. The client will generally accept that the supplier has a legitimate concern about exposure to unspecified types of liability, but the kinds of loss that will flow from a breach of an IT supply contract can be classified, at least in general terms:

- loss of cost or salary savings, or other expected benefits;
- costs of repairing or replacing the defective system;

- costs of additional IT staff and consultants required to make the system work;
- loss of profits resulting from non-performance;
- costs of wasted management time;

These categories of loss are not intended to be definitive: there is no 'definitive list' as such, and each client and supplier will have its own specific concerns. However, the starting point for constructing an effective provision must be to identify the categories of loss that are foreseeable and how the parties intend to allocate these risks between themselves. Any unspecified types of loss will then fall to be determined by the court according to normal legal principles.

ENFORCEABILITY OF EXCLUSION CLAUSES

The contra proferentem rule

An exclusion clause will only operate to limit a party's liability if it covers the breach that has occurred. The rules of interpretation are complicated but in general the more serious the breach of contract, the more clearly-worded the clause must be if it is to exclude liability for that breach: it is interpreted against the person who seeks to rely on it.

One illustration of this rule at work is the case of *Salvage Association v. CAP Financial Services Ltd.* In that case, a contract to supply bespoke software contained a warranty, which also provided that a limitation of liability would apply 'if CAP fails to perform its obligations under [the warranty]'.

The wording of the warranty was sufficiently ambiguous that the court could interpret it as meaning that the warranty did not come into effect until after acceptance of the system by the client. As acceptance had never in fact occurred because the dispute began before the contract's acceptance procedures were reached, the court decided that the warranty never came into effect and so the exclusion of liability never came into effect either. The result was that the supplier's liability for breach of contract was completely unlimited.

The 'reasonableness' test

Under Section 3 of the Unfair Contract Terms Act 1977 (UCTA), where the buyer deals either as a consumer or (if the buyer is a business) on the seller's written standard terms, any exclusion clause favouring the seller must satisfy a test of 'reasonableness' in order to be effective. The measure of 'reasonableness' is whether it was fair and reasonable to include the clause at the time the contract was made. The court will take account of matters such as the following:

- the relative bargaining position of the parties;
- whether the buyer received some benefit (e.g. a lower price) for agreeing to the clause;
- how far the buyer knew or ought to have known of the existence and extent of the clause;
- if the exclusion is contingent on compliance with some condition (e.g. regular maintenance), whether it was reasonable to expect the condition to be complied with;

- whether the goods were specially made or adapted to the client's order.

The courts have also held that the question as to which of the parties can most readily insure against the loss is a relevant consideration and that a limitation of liability is more likely to be reasonable than a complete exclusion.

The Appendix outlines the way in which the courts have applied the UCTA reasonableness test in practice.

Special considerations in software contracts

Computer programs are governed mainly by the law of copyright, which requires that the user of a program has a licence from the copyright owner. (Note that the term 'licence' is synonymous with 'permission' or 'consent'.) There are no particular legal formalities with regard to the form of the licence, but it is desirable for the licence to be in writing to ensure that there is complete clarity as to what may and may not be done with the software. The type of licence depends on the nature of the package:

- Standard software is often supplied by retailers or distributors under a 'shrink-wrap' licence: the disk is wrapped in a clear plastic film, through which the terms of the licence granted by the copyright owner are clearly visible, along with an instruction that breaking the seal on the package will amount to acceptance of those terms.

- Contracts for bespoke software tend to be entered into on a more formal basis, because of the need to agree a specification and to address other issues arising out of the development process. (It may also be the case that the client wishes to own the program outright rather than use it under licence – in which case see the warning in the section on IPRs as to the need for an express assignment of copyright from the contractor.)

The term of the licence may be perpetual or for a fixed period. Again, it is desirable for the term to be spelled out expressly as, in the absence of any express contractual provision, the normal rule is that an intellectual property licence is terminable by 'reasonable notice'.

The licence will often impose restrictions on the use that the client may make of the software. Common restrictions include:

- limiting the number or class of users who may access the software;

- restricting use to the 'internal purposes' of the client (to prevent the client depriving the supplier of potential licence fees by using the software to provide bureau services to third parties);

- prohibiting the client from transferring the software to any third party, again on the basis that the supplier has a right to know precisely who is using its software.

These are all legitimate concerns on the face of it, but the client should check the wording carefully to ensure that the permitted uses reflect all its present and anticipated future requirements. Exceeding the permitted use may leave the client exposed to a claim for copyright infringement or to being charged additional licence fees. At the very least, consider:

- Does this wording prevent the client processing data on behalf of other companies in its group?
- Does the clause operate in such a way as to allow the supplier to impose undefined conditions (such as additional licence fees) in the event of a transfer of the software?
- Might the restriction operate to prevent the client getting a third party to run the system as part of an outsourcing arrangement?

CONCLUSION

The delivery of a working system which meets the client's needs is a difficult enough task, but it is even more difficult to achieve in a contractual vacuum. Clearly, recording each party's contractual obligations and setting up appropriate mechanisms for resolving potential disputes will help to ensure the project stays on track.

APPENDIX: THE 'REASONABLENESS' TEST IN PRACTICE

St Albans City and District Council v. International Computers Ltd

ICL had developed a complex package (COMCIS) to calculate and administer the community charge (or 'poll tax') system of local taxation. St Albans used COMCIS to calculate the number of community charge payers in its area and used that figure to set its community charge rate. The software contained an error, so that although the St Albans database contained all the necessary details, the population figure reported was too high and, as a result, St Albans suffered a financial loss.

The contract contained a clause limiting ICL's liability to the price or charge payable for the item of equipment, program or service in respect of which the liability arose or £100000 (whichever was the lesser) and completely excluding liability for any indirect or consequential loss or loss of business or profits sustained by the client. Liability turned on whether this clause was reasonable under UCTA.

ICL contested that UCTA applied at all, arguing that the contract had not been on standard terms. However, the judge held that UCTA did apply: in other words, that St Albans had contracted on ICL's written standard terms. Even though many elements of the contract were negotiated at length (e.g. delivery dates and specification), ICL's General Conditions (which contained the limitation and exclusion clauses) 'remained effectively untouched in the negotiations', and indeed were referred to by ICL staff as 'Standard Terms and Conditions' in witness statements and letters.

The court then went on to consider whether the exclusions were 'reasonable' and concluded that they were not. Although St Albans knew of the limitation and had attempted to negotiate it, the following factors operated to render the clause unreasonable:

- ICL had substantially more resources than St Albans;
- ICL held product liability insurance in an aggregate sum of £50 million worldwide;
- ICL called no evidence to show that the limitation to £100 000 was reasonable, either in relation to the potential risk or the actual loss;
- the contract had mistakenly been made on an outmoded version of the General Conditions; in the then current version, the standard limitation had been increased to £125 000;
- local authorities are not in the same position as private sector businesses: their operations are constrained by statute and financial restraints and they cannot necessarily be expected to insure against commercial risks;
- St. Albans received no inducement to agree to the limitation and there was evidence that all ICL's competitors imposed similar limitations of liability;
- when St Albans tried to negotiate the limitation, albeit at the last moment, ICL in effect said that this was not possible because it would delay the provision of the software to St Albans beyond the date for implementation of the community charge.

The judge accordingly found that ICL had not discharged its burden of proving that the term was fair and reasonable and also that financially ICL was better placed to bear a risk of this kind through insurance and spread it across its client base.

South West Water Services Ltd v. International Computers Ltd

SWW and ICL had entered into two contracts – a turnkey agreement and a project management agreement – under which ICL was to deliver a client service system to SWW. After ICL accepted that it would be unable to deliver the system to specification and in accordance with a planned timetable, SWW sued for breach of contract, claiming that ICL had failed to deliver the system as agreed, and for misrepresentation.

Both agreements had contained a clause based on a standard ICL contract and purporting to limit ICL's liability for any claim for loss or damage. The evidence was that, during the negotiations, SWW had originally submitted its own standard procurement conditions to ICL and that ICL had rejected them.

The question then arose whether, in these circumstances, the ICL limitations could be regarded as ICL's 'standard terms'. The court followed the *St Albans* decision in finding that, even though SWW originally offered its own terms in negotiations, in the event ICL had dealt on ICL's standard terms which had been only slightly adapted. The fact that one fairly predictable eventuality – failure to progress the project to a point where there was a system in place for SWW that was capable of being tested – had not been addressed in the documentation also tended to suggest that the contract should be regarded as 'standard terms'.

The judge went on to note that the extent to which a party has had discussions and has freely entered into a contract on the other party's standard terms may be relevant as an important circumstance in considering whether those terms are reasonable. ICL argued that its standard limitation clause should be treated as reasonable in this case because its terms had been subject to arm's length discussion and negotiations, but this was found not be the case on the evidence.

This contribution is based on the author's chapter on System Procurement Contracts, in the 5th edition of Computer Law (2003), published by Oxford University Press.

3 Implementing New Systems

JEAN MORGAN

This chapter considers some of the issues which can and have arisen in the purchase and implementation of new systems. It also reviews the role of IT systems in a merger or acquisition and describes a method for IT due diligence which can help to avoid the pitfalls.

INTRODUCTION

When Mick Jagger sang 'I Can't Get No Satisfaction' in 1965, computers were only just starting to make an appearance in business. Nearly 40 years on, the influence of computers is all-pervasive. And when they go wrong, in extreme cases, the business can go wrong. We first heard in the early 1980s that a business had gone into liquidation as the direct result of a failed computer implementation. More recently, the technology underpinning the www.boo.com website was highlighted as one of the contributory causes for its business failure. One major corporation saw its share price fall in 2001 when it admitted that its computer systems had become 'dated' and were in need of complete overhaul. In less extreme cases, disputes arise which monopolize managers' attention for far too long, and may result in long and expensive court cases with no winner. Some recent examples include:

- A new computer system that does not do what the supplier said it would.
- An ecommerce website that crashes when more than six people access it.
- A software package that is still not in production three years after it was purchased.
- A bespoke software module that one company paid for but which the supplier is now selling to other clients.
- A system that does not work and from which the data cannot be extracted to move into a replacement system.
- A new system that requires expensive consultancy to make it usable.
- A website that seems to be down more than it is up.
- A new system that will not talk to the network, which must now be upgraded.

- A system on which the client wants more acceptance testing but which the supplier says is complete.
- Software on which the client wants changes but for which the supplier is asking a large price.
- A company acquires a smaller company but the supplier wants a lot more money for the acquisition to use the parent company's systems.
- A system that is proving very difficult and expensive to link with that of a key client.
- A supplier which says that remote working cannot be done (cost-effectively).

Chapter 12 deals with dispute resolution. Prevention is clearly better than cure.

SETTING REALISTIC EXPECTATIONS

There is frequently a major mismatch between what a client expects the IT system to do and what it actually will do. This may be the result of a salesman who sets client expectations too high or it may be the result of golf course chat: a company director is told about a competitor's successful new system and wants it for his firm. Computer systems are often sold as promises, salesware or vapourware, but bear in mind a transport firm's van display, 'A promise is nothing until it's delivered'. If there is a suspicion that the system does not exist or is not yet implemented, then it is essential to insist on seeing some evidence of the promises before embarking on an enhanced due diligence exercise.

A public sector project ran into major difficulties when it procured a software package from a long-established supplier. First, it accepted assurances that this version of the software, specially amended for the public sector, had been implemented elsewhere. It had not; although an implementation was underway, it had already overrun its schedule several times. Secondly, the project had decided it wanted a browser-based version of the software. Salespeople may describe this as a small matter of adding a new front end. In practice, much of the software had to be re-written and, again, the outcome was major delays through the need for additional testing.

Where the system does exist in some form at the time of sale, many buyers still choose the system based only on a demonstration by the sales people. It is very easy indeed to build a shell of a system which appears to do what you want, but which is actually just a shell, enhanced by smoke and mirrors. Computer sales people are often as effective as a magician at convincing the potential buyer that he or she has witnessed something that will be business-enhancing. Remember, though, that such demonstrations show the points that the seller wishes to show, often the glamorous and interesting aspects, and they show the parts of the system that do work. It is still rare for the buyer to take control of the situation and impose an agenda on the seller which homes in on the aspects of the system which are most important to the buyer.

This agenda-based approach requires that the buyer has some knowledge of the package market before embarking on the search: the method works by spending little time and effort on the areas of software that all packages of that type should have and it invests most effort on the areas that will give the business competitive advantage. This approach can unsettle some vendors, but it has major advantages for the buyer. It focuses on how the software will meet the business needs, reduces the scope for the supplier to mislead the buyer, and improves the ability to compare competing solutions. It will also feed directly into a specification which can be referenced in the contract for the purchase. Suppliers can be less keen because it demands a higher investment in the sales effort. To help to mitigate this effect, buyers should filter out the least suitable suppliers before a very short short-list is subjected to deeper scrutiny.

This method worked very successfully, for example, with a recent procurement of ERP software and accounting software for a project-based business. In the ERP exercise, four suppliers were short-listed for two-day demonstration sessions which used the client's agenda for 90% of the time; the suppliers were given the opportunity to show off the features that they chose only during the final session. The buyer remained very much in control of the situation and achieved a positive relationship with all four suppliers. A further fringe benefit for the buyer's organization was the team building and buy-in that was achieved in the project team, as a result of the time spent working together on the supplier road show.

SPECIFYING THE CORRECT REQUIREMENT

Many people still labour under the impression that computer systems will, by themselves, solve problems. If an IT investment is made in a hurry and without following a well-proven approach, then the resultant computer system may just automate the existing problems or make them occur faster, or it may bring additional problems of its own! The biggest problems arise when either the wrong solution is chosen at the beginning or when the implementation is poorly executed.

Gartner Group concluded, in 2002, that UK businesses waste £23bn every year on IT, equivalent to 20% of the country's combined IT budget. Wasted money is often the result of rushing headlong into an inappropriate computer solution. Many IT departments subscribe to structured methods which provide for a Business Scoping or Feasibility Study phase, and yet this work is often by-passed because of political pressure from a key stakeholder who believes that he knows what the solution is. This chapter is not the place to discuss how to manage the often-messy initiation stage of a project, but a pragmatic business study with requirements specification is a key preventive measure in avoiding future IT pitfalls.

Ian Alexander, an independent consultant and committee member of the BCS Requirements Engineering Specialist Group, summarized the principal aspects of a robust set of requirements. In many projects, this checklist has proved to be very useful guidance.

- Each requirement must stand alone.
- Each requirement must specify exactly one thing.
- Each requirement must be verifiable.
- Each requirement must be necessary.
- Each requirement must be realistic.
- User requirements must state what the user wants.
- System requirements must state what the system must do.
- The users must own their requirements.
- All requirements must be reviewed.

There is additional guidance in the DSDM Framework which recommends that requirements be categorized and prioritized with the MoSCoW guide (DSDM 1997):

- Must have: requirements that are fundamental to the project's success. Without them the system will be unworkable and useless. These requirements define the minimum usable subset. A DSDM project guarantees to satisfy the minimum usable subset.
- Should have: important requirements for which there is a workaround in the short term. They would be classed as mandatory in a less time-constrained development but the system will be useful and usable without them.
- Could have: requirements that can more easily be left out of the increment under development.
- Want to have but will not have this time round: valuable requirements that can wait until later development.

A good set of requirements forms the foundation of successful acceptance testing, which has massive significance (see Chapter 2). This should serve to emphasize the importance of thinking through, and documenting, the system requirements.

A survey (Bishop Fleming 2002) questioned 1500 businesses in South West England with a turnover greater than £2 million. More than half of the companies had experienced problems with a new system soon after installation. 40% of respondents concluded that the single thing they would do differently would be to 'take more time to specify our requirements'.

SCOPING THE PROJECT

Once the software has been chosen, there is still plenty that can go wrong.

There is often a need to commission some new hardware and network capacity that the software will require. Great care has to be taken to estimate the size of these correctly: too small and the system will grind to a halt when your business is most busy; too large and you'll end up paying too much for it. This was one of the main causes of wasted money in the Gartner report of 2002 mentioned above. Some commentators suggest that the slump in IT spending in 2002–3 was partly caused by companies which bought too much capacity to cover themselves for work on the millennium (or Year 2000) bug and then spent the following couple of years using up that capacity.

The supplier of the software can help with the specification of the implementation requirements, although it is often worth having a review by an independent expert. Conflicts of interest may arise if the supplier thinks that budgets are tight and there may be pressure to buy hardware that is only just big enough, rather than allowing for business growth. System sizing is a specialist skill and needs to be taken seriously.

Many systems now require extensive 'configuration' before they can be used. The software may be installed but it can take a significant amount of time to tailor the software to fit your business. Some ERP implementations take over 18 months for this tailoring; the software as it comes 'out of the wrapper' is built in a modular fashion and has to be fitted together based on your business rules. Make sure that your timetable allows for this and that you have committed enough of your staff to achieve it – it can be very intensive and time-consuming.

PLANNING

The arrival of a new system is an exciting time. If your business has prepared properly for it, the implementation can be almost painless, but there is a lot to coordinate and it is easy to overlook some of the details. The Case Study illustrates some of the pitfalls that can occur.

A specialist project manager will have experience of many system implementations and you should weigh up the risks of not appointing one against the cost of engaging one or appointing a qualified member of staff to take on the responsibility. The project manager will plan and execute the implementation, while ensuring that an appropriate risk assessment is in place to protect your business. There will be formal checkpoints at which all of the stakeholders can understand how complete the plan is and what future actions are required. The project manager should also be experienced in contract and vendor management, which will encourage a positive relationship with the supplier and his staff. When the implementation is complete, the project manager should undertake a proper handover of any remaining responsibilities from the supplier to your own staff.

CASE STUDY

This example illustrates what can go wrong in a computer system implementation. Although it dates from a few years ago, the issues are timeless.

AB was a highly successful West Midlands goods processing company that added attractive packaging and value to bulk goods and split them up into individual units or small groups of units for sale. To improve client response and minimize the time that goods spent on the shop floor, i.e. to optimize the use of workspace, it ordered a computer-aided production management system. Its objective was to more closely control the allocation of incoming goods to the staff who would pack or adjust or add value to prepare them for sale.

The operations within the company were very labour-intensive and at times several hundreds of staff worked on conveyor lines, converting incoming goods into outgoing, packed items. Their work was controlled manually by 26 production scheduling staff who monitored orders, the arrival of incoming goods, and the flow of goods along the conveyor lines and into vehicles for despatch to various market outlets. In view of the fact that the nature of the work carried out was labour-intensive using relatively unskilled labour, this trading sector is extremely competitive. The key to success is very rapid turnaround of incoming goods to maintain goodwill with clients and minimize the time between arrival of incoming goods and their despatch for marketing and sale, in order to speed up the corresponding cash flow.

The computer-aided production management system was ordered several months before its arrival and was scheduled to arrive approximately one month before it actually did arrive. In order to justify the costs of the system, the production scheduling staff were given one month's notice of redundancy which was issued for the promised time of delivery of the computer system; this was so that one month's parallel running of the manual and computer systems would be possible. In the event, delivery of the system was one month late. Therefore, the overlap between manual production scheduling, by disillusioned staff who were being made redundant, and the incoming computer system was only three days. No exhaustive parallel running could be carried out to check consistency between manual and computer scheduling.

Four days after the production scheduling staff had left the company and some seven days into the operation of the new computer system, a 'logic bomb' or bug in the software zeroed all the data files. Virtually all the input information relating to clients, products in progress and future orders was totally lost. The system was new and the member of staff operating it had not been taught to take backups, and therefore recovery was not possible. Neither was it possible to revert to the manual system since the staff who operated it had left.

The net result was chaos. Goods which were supposed to flow along the company's production lines (typically, the time between receipt and departure was within 48 hours) ceased to move since there were no schedules to establish and progress the movement! Clients became disillusioned when their goods did not arrive. Within 48 hours virtually all the incoming goods which had arrived for processing were taken to competitors for processing, as were future orders.

The origin of the 'logic bomb' was never determined since the company went into liquidation some days after it lost the major part of its business. The problem may have been a deliberate 'logic bomb' put in by an aggrieved member of staff about to depart, or by a competitor, or by someone within the systems house which had produced the system, although the latter seems most unlikely. With no funds available for detailed investigation, no one knows whether it was accidental or deliberate.

Since continuous production scheduling is crucial to such a company, diversion of middle and senior management to the shop floor could have saved the company. No such contingency plans were ever formulated and it went into liquidation.

REALIZING BENEFITS

Just because the system is live, do not assume that you can sit back. This is when the full effect of the IT investment can be seen and when your dependence on the new system will become evident. Make sure that you have business continuity plans in place and that you have tested your disaster recovery plans so that everyone knows what to do should disaster strike. You should also check that your security policy is working and amend it as required.

As your business becomes fully used to the new system, you may find that you want to make changes or improvements to it. Perhaps these relate to some of the lower priority requirements that were 'MoSCoWed' out of the first delivery. These changes will need to be scoped, specified and managed in much the same way as the main system implementation, even if with a slightly lighter touch. Many businesses plan to have a post-implementation review, when the stakeholders get together to plan future changes; this may be six, nine or 12 months after the initial implementation. It is recommended as a useful opportunity to stand back from the day-to-day running of the system and to take stock of the situation. The supplier may contribute to the review by sharing development plans for the software.

IT IN MERGERS AND ACQUISITIONS

While most businesses will make their major IT investment through purchase of a new system, if your business is merging with another or is acquiring a business, then the IT risks and issues must be reviewed within the overall due diligence exercise which is normally undertaken. Options such as integrating the two companies' IT systems or replacing one company's systems with those of the other need to be considered as a means of achieving economy of scale. Ensure that your software licences enable this extension of scope and that there are termination clauses in the contract for the software that you will replace. Whichever way you choose to go, the implementation will need to be properly planned and the risk assessed.

IT DUE DILIGENCE

Terry White (2001) re-thought the role of the IT department. He learned from some bad experiences that 'due diligence investigations should ... be a prerequisite investigation of any major IT acquisition'. A typical due diligence exercise will include many aspects. With experience, the potential purchaser will determine which elements may be omitted or played down and which elements should be given extra emphasis. For example, if the package you are looking at will be fundamental to your future business, then the due diligence exercise will need to be thorough and extensive, while for a less critical supply or for a commodity system, the due diligence can be tailored down. You also need to ensure that the right people partic-ipate in the exercise. The scepticism of your more cynical colleagues is valuable in due diligence, where only seeing is believing and evidence is all.

One of the most enlightening aspects of due diligence is to take some ref-erences from existing clients. The suspicion is that the supplier will provide a list of 'tame' clients, but it is absolutely worth making the telephone calls to references. Existing clients are often forthright and enable you to build up a picture of the supplier's post-sales service.

The most successful outcome of due diligence comes from taking a holis-tic approach. Each aspect is important and if there are major concerns in any one area, it can scupper the whole agreement. The project can still fail up to the point that the due diligence is complete, and your business should have an alternative plan of action to follow if due diligence highlights too many risks.

The outcome of a well-executed due diligence exercise is a better negoti-ating position, with fewer unknowns and reduced risk.

IT DUE DILIGENCE INVESTIGATIONS

- Investigate the supplier's background and financial standing. Do some basic number crunching on the supplier's financial accounts and management accounts.

- Look at the supplier's capability for support. This will include people, resources, methods of working, processes used, production and delivery methods. Does the supplier have enough staff to support your implementation? Will they be working on other implemen-tations at the same time? Understand how the supplier's Help Desk operates. What is the supplier's track record like? How fair are the standard terms of business? Ask for evidence of all claims made by the supplier. Understand escrow arrangements.

- Consider the product's positioning in the market, the sales potential and the competitive situation. If a product does not have a sound future, the supplier may not continue to develop and support it as you would wish. Ensure that the supplier's plans for the prod-uct fit with your IT strategy and security policy. Compatibility of systems is often down-played by suppliers – trying to fit together a new system and an existing system can be the worst nightmare, so it is far better to check it out beforehand.

- Review the implementation services which the supplier should supply, e.g. consultancy and training, and determine whether they suit your requirements.

- Define exactly what is included in the agreed price and what is not. If the system is config-urable, then ensure that responsibilities are clear as to how much the supplier can do and how much your staff should do. Get estimates of travel expenses, which can make a big dif-ference to the end cost. Who will do the training and what facilities are required? How will change control work if you want some system processing amended? How will you do acceptance testing? Does the supplier deem the system to be accepted if testing is not complete within a certain amount of time? What are the terms, e.g. time and materials or fixed price?

- Take references from existing clients. Do not stint on the reference calls. They are an opportunity to substantiate many of the claims which the supplier may have made.

- Review the draft contract terms early. How many contracts will there be? Often there are separate contracts for the system, the implementation services and the on-going support. It is essential to make sure that the separate contracts fit together when taken as a whole. Make sure that the agreed price is still as expected when all the aspects are taken together. Clarify the extent of warranties and liabilities. What are the termination clauses? Ensure that all of the software that you will use within the new system will be properly licensed to you and that ownership of all IPR is clear. How are the licenses and fees structured if your business grows by buying another company? What happens if you decide to outsource your IT support? How is problem management to take place? Are there escalation routes?

- Review the steps you may take if things go wrong. Some contracts now include scope for mediation and alternative dispute resolution services, as a means of resolving disputes and discouraging litigation.

CONCLUSIONS

When an IT implementation goes according to plan, everyone wins: the supplier is happy and may gain a reference site and the company is happy as its business is working more effectively. Sadly, though, there are many opportunities for things to go wrong in systems implementation projects and the impact of system failures inevitably falls on the business.

REFERENCES

Alexander, I., and Stevens, R. (2002) *Writing Better Requirements.* Addison-Wesley.

Bishop Fleming (2002) Available at www.bishopfleming.co.uk.

DSDM Consortium (1997) *Dynamic Systems Development Method Version 3.* Tesseract Publishing.

Gartner Group (2002) in *Computing,* 15 March 2002.

White, T. (2001) *Reinventing the IT Department.* Oxford: Butterworth-Heinemann.

4 Avoiding Employment Problems

JEREMY HOLT

This chapter discusses policies for the use of email and computers and the health and safety requirements with which an employer must comply. Each section ends with an action plan and the appendix contains a specimen policy.

INTRODUCTION

Employees can cause their employers all manner of problems in their use of computers and email. For example:

- Misuse of computer systems can waste staff time and leave businesses (and their management) exposed to claims for discrimination, harassment, defamation or worse.

- Failure to include proper business information in electronic communications can result in criminal liability under the Companies Act.

- Stringent health and safety requirements about the quality of screens and other computer equipment used by staff must be met.

COMPUTER AND EMAIL USAGE POLICIES

An employer can be held responsible for wrongful actions carried out by employees in the course of their employment. This is the case even if the act is done in a way that has not been authorized by the employer. For example, an employer can be held responsible for employees' acts involving racial and sexual harassment, downloading pornography, defamation of management, customers or competitors, breach of confidence, copyright infringement, hacking and breaches of the Data Protection Act.

To provide staff with some guidance and avoid these problems, employers have adopted computer use and email policies. More than half of all businesses in the US now have such policies, but every business is different and no single policy will suit all.

Employers should also remember that, in certain cases, both the employer and the employee are liable for the employee's wrongful action. It can be useful to remind employees of this in order to encourage them to comply with rules forbidding particular conduct.

The problem with email

Users adopt a more relaxed manner when using email, similar to a telephone conversation rather than a letter. However, the form of the communication is much more permanent and it can be stored and passed on very easily. The thoughts of an employee expressed in an email could be critical later when used to defend, or damage, their employer in legal proceedings. Two graphic examples of what can go wrong come from large firms of solicitors in London (who should really know better). In one, a male solicitor received an email from his (then) girlfriend commenting favourably on their most recent sexual encounter. The explicit content of the email ensured that copies of it were passed on in a chain reaction to millions of people within weeks. In another case, which involved a race discrimination claim, a throwaway comment from the employer about the ideal physical attributes of any new secretary (which was somehow passed on to the claimant, a former secretary, who did not have such attributes) brought a great deal of unwanted publicity to the firm concerned.

Two points should be emphasized. First, if these comments had been spoken (or even expressed in a written letter which would have been much more difficult to copy and pass on to a large number of people), they would not have caused the trouble that they did. Secondly, the damage to the employer is more likely to be to their public reputation than financially, particularly if the comments expressed are sexual or discriminatory in some way.

The problem that the storage of emails can cause was highlighted in the celebrated Oliver North case in America. Although Oliver North had thought that he could completely delete certain computer data, such data was retrieved by the authorities and used as evidence against him. It is surprising how effective a good computer forensic company can be. In another case a drug dealer was convicted because he had stored details of his drug transactions on his handheld computer and, although he believed that they had been deleted, they were retrieved by the police.

An email message is stored in a number of places – the sender's machine, the recipient's machine and (because of the technical manner in which email messages are transmitted across the internet) the machines of any other people to whom it may have been copied. As a result, it is extremely difficult to destroy all records of a message sent.

Staff should be discouraged from commenting by email on any legal dispute in which their employer is involved, in case such comments are used against the employer later in legal proceedings.

Monitoring emails and internet use

Employers sometimes wonder whether they have the right to monitor voice calls or email messages and there are a number of myths about this. For a start, there is no legal distinction between phone calls, faxes and email messages for these purposes; all telecommunications are treated the same and the same rules apply to each medium.

The basic principle (set out in the Regulation of Investigatory Powers Act

2000) is that telecommunications may not be intercepted by employers unless both the sender and the recipient have consented to the interception. Indeed it is a criminal offence for employers to carry out unauthorized interception and, if they do, they face up to two years' imprisonment and/or a fine, as well as the possibility of an injunction or damages claim.

However, under a separate set of regulations (snappily entitled the Telecommunications (Lawful Business Practice) (Interception of Communications) Regulations 2000), businesses are allowed to intercept communications without consent in certain limited circumstances. To take advantage of these exceptions, the messages must relate to the business and be on a system provided in connection with the business. The exceptions include:

- establishing the existence of facts (e.g. recording transactions in case there is a contractual dispute);
- compliance with regulatory standards;
- detecting crime (e.g. fraud or corruption);
- investigating unauthorized use of the system (e.g. to check that company rules on emails or internet use are being followed);
- checking on the standards of people using the system (e.g. for quality control or staff training);
- protecting the system from viruses or other threats to the system;
- backing up or rerouting emails when a member of staff is on holiday or off sick.

Employers are required to take all reasonable steps to notify users that interception may take place. This is relatively easy with employees as it can be stated in a staff policy. However, it is much more difficult with outsiders sending inbound emails. One method of notification is in outbound email and fax disclaimers. Employers should remember that even if interception of messages is carried out by them in a legitimate manner, any use by them of the information gathered must be proportionate and in accordance with the Data Protection Act (see Chapter 9).

In June 2003, the Information Commissioner published a code on monitoring at work. Although this code does not have the force of law it will be used in any enforcement action by the Information Commissioner and may be referred to in employment tribunal proceedings. The code emphasizes that monitoring of messages should only take place when there is a real business need and the methods used should not be unduly intrusive into an employee's privacy. Employees have a reasonable expectation that they can keep their personal lives private which means that they are entitled to some privacy at work. It is recommended that employers should wherever possible avoid opening emails, especially ones that clearly show that they are private or personal. Employees should be aware that monitoring is taking place and told the reasons for it and the means used. Covert monitoring will only be legitimate in the most exceptional of circumstances such as the detection of crime or equivalent wrongdoing. It is good practice for the monitoring to be carried out by someone other than the employee's line manager e.g. Security or Human Resources personnel. In this way, personal information that is picked up can be sifted so that only the most relevant information becomes known to those who work with the employee.

Laying down a policy for staff

All businesses should draw up a policy for staff on their use of computers (and access to the internet, if applicable) and notify all staff of it. Unless it is wildly unreasonable, staff cannot argue about such a policy. Their use of the employer's equipment is conditional upon their following the policy laid down, otherwise they can be in serious trouble. The policy should be emphasized during the induction of new staff. A specimen staff computer use policy is shown in the Appendix at the end of this chapter. Note that this policy should not just be restricted to employees; it should also be given to outside contractors and agency staff.

The policy can be backed up by reminders on computer screens and regular training. Internal audits should check that security policies are being followed and the side should not be let down by senior management (as it frequently is). The aim should be that no user of the firm's computers could reasonably argue that they were not aware of the rules for the use of them.

Private email

It is unrealistic for employers to ban completely the private use of email by employees. No doubt the same discussions took place when the telephone first started to be used widely within business. A recent survey of businesses using email found that the vast majority allowed the sending of private emails but subject to certain conditions. These included the messages being kept short and their only being sent during break time.

If private email use is allowed, it is critical that such messages be sent in an appropriate format and that they not appear to be official messages from the company. The best way to do this is in the signature section of the message. There should be two different formats for the employee to use depending on whether the message is official or private e.g. 'This message is from Jeremy Holt and is sent in a private capacity'. The next section discusses the signature for business emails. The importance of differentiating between the two kinds of messages, official and private, can be seen if employees send messages to newsgroups or bulletin boards.

Some employers allow employees to set up private web-based email accounts for private emails. In this case, the employer can not monitor such messages and the messages sent do not use the employer's return address.

Website access

The policy prohibiting staff visits to unauthorized sites (e.g. pornographic or recruitment agency sites) can be reinforced by the use of filtering systems and blocking software (which is surprisingly inexpensive). In the writer's experience, just the knowledge by the staff that such blocking software is being used is enough to reduce significantly visits to unauthorized sites during work time. Obviously, staff may visit them from their home computers but this does not waste valuable working time.

It is surprising how tough Employment Tribunals are prepared to be about the dismissal of employees for downloading of pornography, particularly if there is a policy in force forbidding this. One question that is often asked in these circumstances is whether employers are required to notify the police. Generally the police are not generally interested unless the pornography is being sold by the employee or it involves children.

There is no doubt that employers can dismiss staff for excessive surfing of the web during working hours. In 1999, a computer manager at a firm of management consultants was dismissed fairly for using the office computer to do 150 searches for cheap holiday deals. Whilst it may not be practical for employers to check what sites employees have been visiting, peer group pressure does work. If other employees are having to work harder because one is surfing the web, the employer is soon likely to hear about it.

Hacking

Some astute employers give new employees a copy of the Computer Misuse Act 1990 when they start (they cost £3.40 each from Stationery Office Limited. The Computer Misuse Act makes it a criminal offence to use, access or alter another person's computer without prior permission.

Disclaimers on business emails

Businesses sometimes believe that all their ills can be cured by a well-drafted disclaimer at the foot of an email. Email disclaimers are of little value other than to notify the recipient that the contents of the email are confidential and to offer a method of reporting any misdirection. Email disclaimers are no substitute either for a proper staff email policy or for the legal information that must be shown in an email which is the same as must be shown on a business letter (see box).

INFORMATION REQUIRED ON BUSINESS LETTERS

The following information must appear on company letters:
- the full name of the company;
- the registered number of the company;
- the address of the registered office and an indication that that address is the registered office;
- the country of registration of the company.

For partnerships of 20 or fewer partners, the names of the partners and an address for service must appear. Partnerships of more than 20 may simply say that a list of the partners is available at a particular address.

Sole traders must have their real name (i.e. not just a trading name) and an address on their business letters.

Businesses who do not abide by these rules risk looking amateur or newly-started (or both).

There is no reason to differentiate between a letter sent by post and a letter sent by email. Most businesses are failing to follow these rules fully in relation to emails at the moment. This is all the more surprising when the vast majority of business messages are now sent by email rather than by formal business letter. There are a number of consequences of failing to abide by the Companies Act 1985 and the Business Names Act 1985 in providing the required information in company letters or emails:

- It is a criminal offence both by the company concerned and by the person who authorizes the communication on behalf of the company.

- If the communication relates to an order for goods and the company's name is not mentioned in the email, the individual who sent it can be personally liable for the order.

- Difficulties can arise in bringing legal proceedings to enforce a contract made where the appropriate information has not appeared on the company's notepaper or in the company's email.

Action plan on computer use

- Introduce a computer use and email policy. If there is no policy, an employer can not monitor what is happening except in very limited circumstances.

- Make sure that such a policy is notified to all employees and contractors and that they are reminded of it from time to time (e.g. by banner warnings when logging on to the system), otherwise it will not be possible to rely on it later just when it is needed.

- Ensure that all emails contain the correct business information. Devise a system whereby personal emails from members of staff are clearly differentiated from emails on company business.

AVOIDING HEALTH AND SAFETY CLAIMS

Health and safety legislation rears its head in relation to the use of computers by staff. Most businesses use computers now and it is critically important to be aware of the health and safety aspects. Failure to abide by such rules can lead to either imprisonment or a fine, in addition to the inevitable bad publicity. It also leaves the door open for personal injury claims from present (or, more likely, past) employees. For example, there are well over 200 000 repetitive strain injury (RSI) claims in the UK each year. RSI is now known as 'upper limb disorders in the workplace'.

The law on health and safety at work

There are general duties on all employers under the Health and Safety at Work etc. Act 1974 and the Management of Health and Safety at Work Regulations 1999 that require the risks to health that may be associated with work to be addressed. In addition, the health risks in relation to work with display screen equipment (DSE) are covered by the Health and Safety (Display Screen Equipment) Regulations 1992 and the Health and Safety Executive (HSE) publishes specific guidance on the subject. Duty holders must comply with the DSE Regulations and guidance. The HSE published the revised HSG 60 'Upper Limb Disorders in the Workplace' in 2002.

The DSE Regulations

The DSE Regulations apply to anyone who regularly uses display screen equipment (which includes screens that display text, numbers or graphics) whether at the work site, off site or in a home-based office. An evaluation of display screen use must be carried out, including an assessment of all work-stations. The requirements are in the form of general targets rather than technical specifications:

- Screens should be flicker-free as far as is possible; brightness and con-trast should be adjustable. The screen height and angle should also be adjustable allowing operators to avoid glare and maintain a natural and relaxed posture.
- The keyboard should be designed to allow operators to locate and use keys quickly, accurately and without discomfort. (Some employers offer staff a choice of keyboards such as the Microsoft, ergonomic or 'Cherry' styles.)
- The height of the work surface, the work chair and, if necessary, the foot rest should all be adjustable to allow the user to achieve a com-fortable position.
- Lighting should be appropriate for the tasks performed and reflections and glare reduced to a minimum.
- Background noise should be kept at a level which does not impair nor-mal conversation. Normal conversation is regarded as the ability to hold a conversation up to two metres apart without raising the voice.
- Ventilation and humidity should be maintained at levels which pre-vent discomfort and problems of sore eyes.

- Software must be suitable for the task, easy to use and display information in a format and at a pace which are adapted to users.
- Software must not contain quantitative or qualitative checking facilities of which the user is unaware.

The Regulations give users the right to eye tests for display screen work, at the cost of the employer. A user can request a test when they first become a user and at regular intervals afterwards. If the tests show that the user requires spectacles or contact lenses for VDU work, then the employer is responsible for the cost of providing one pair of basic spectacles or contact lenses.

Action plan on health and safety

To stay out of trouble employers should do the following:

- Assess which workstations require analysis and conduct an appropriate audit to ensure compliance with the minimum requirements.
- Consult with employees to discuss health and safety issues as well as their working environment and set up a reporting procedure to respond to any problems.
- Inform staff of their rights concerning eye tests and the provision of glasses or contact lenses.
- Arrange appropriate training for staff in their use of their workstations and equipment.
- Keep a 'paper trail' of all the actions taken by the employer in order to provide a defence against any future personal injury claims by employees.
- Carry out pre-employment health screening, effective sickness absence management and exit health screening to ensure employees' fitness and capabilities for work.
- Be aware of the requirements of the Disability Discrimination Act 1995 e.g. providing modifications and adaptations for staff deemed disabled. The Disability Employment Advisor from the local Placement and Counselling Team in the Employment Service can assist in this.
- Vary work activities and ensure adequate breaks from work and between tasks.

In short, there is no antidote for employers against an RSI claim. Employers can only reduce the risk of successful claims by meeting health and safety obligations, in particular concentrating on posture, ergonomics and working methods.

If you find all this rather tedious and you would like help, ask an occupational health professional. They can provide you with useful advice (beyond simply the minimum legal requirements), such as ways to help staff to avoid back problems. To find an occupational health professional ring the HSE Information Line who will give you the details of your local HSE office and the

Employment Medical Advisory Service (EMAS). Although they cannot make individual recommendations they can provide you with details of providers in your area. Occupational health professionals are more likely than lawyers to know the Health and Safety regulations and they are far cheaper.

APPENDIX: SPECIMEN POLICY FOR COMPUTER AND EMAIL USE

We do not wish to restrict in any way your use of our computer system – indeed we encourage it. However we regard the integrity of our computer system as key to the success of our business. To avoid misunderstanding and confusion all employees must abide by the following policies. Breaches of this policy will be taken seriously and could amount to gross misconduct. You should direct any queries about this policy to the Human Resources Department.

Licensed software

Only properly licensed software may be loaded onto our system. You are not allowed to use within the company any material that you either know, or suspect to be, in breach of copyright. In addition, you are not allowed to pass such material on to anyone else. It is important to bear in mind that breach of copyright for business purposes can be a criminal offence both by the company and by the individual concerned. No software may be loaded onto our system without first obtaining the express permission of the IT Department. Software includes business applications, shareware, entertainment software, games, screensavers, and demonstration software. If you are unsure whether a piece of software requires a licence, please contact the IT Department. The copying of software media and manuals is also prohibited.

Networks

You are not allowed to make any change to the connection or configuration of your PC. None of our PCs may be connected to a customer's network without permission from the IT Department and written permission from the customer concerned. In addition, none of our PCs may be connected to a public network, e.g. the internet, without permission from the IT Department.

Disks

You must not use disks from unknown sources or from home computers. All data disks must be virus-checked before they may be used on our computer system.

Viruses

Generally, more damage to files is caused by inappropriate corrective action than by viruses themselves. If a virus is suspected you should do nothing more until instructed. The matter must be reported immediately to the IT Department. The most likely way that our computer system will be infected by a virus is from an external message. Any outside material must be properly virus-checked before being loaded on to our computer system. Many viruses are now spread by email messages and use the address book of the recipient to pass it on to other people. Some of these viruses are activated when an attachment to the message is opened. Creators of these viruses frequently encourage the user to open the attachment simply by using a header such as 'You must read this!' You should not open any attachment of this type and must generally be suspicious of any message that is received from an unknown source. In other words, only open mail when you know it is from a reliable source. If you receive email warnings about viruses please ignore the instructions they contain. In the majority of cases they are hoaxes and the instructions, if followed, will damage our computer system.

Customer procedures

If you use a customer's computer system you must observe the customer's rules relating to their computers. In the absence of any such rules, our rules should be followed.

Access

You are only allowed access to those parts of our computer system which you need in order to carry out your normal duties.

Inappropriate material

You must not view or download or pass on any pornographic material on our computer system or place obscene or offensive screensavers on your PC. In line with the normal rules that apply to you as an employee, you are not allowed to send racist, sexist, blasphemous, defamatory, obscene, indecent or abusive messages on our computer system, either internally or externally. Do think carefully before sending any questionable messages that could reflect badly on us as a company.

Use of the internet at work

The primary reason for our providing you with access to the internet and/or email is to assist you in your work for us. You are allowed to send personal emails in a similar way to the way that minor incidental personal telephone use is allowed. Such activity should not be excessive and must not affect your ability to work properly for us during normal working hours. Personal emails should be kept to a minimum and the company's footer MUST NOT be shown on a personal email.

You are not allowed to go onto the internet for your own purposes during normal working hours. You are allowed to do so outside normal working hours (and during your lunch hour).

You are not allowed to send unsolicited emails or emails to multiple recipients or to use email for personal gain. You are also not allowed to use the company's internet access and email system to sign up for online shopping or internet membership schemes or chat rooms.

Business emails

You must not order anything on our behalf by email without proper authorization. You should always bear in mind that an email from the company has the same legal effect as a letter from the company on the company's notepaper. This underlines the importance of being careful with what you say in an email in case it is misunderstood. All company emails must contain our standard footer which will be notified to you from time to time. As stated above, personal emails must not contain the company's standard footer.

Confidentiality

Before sending any confidential information by email consider carefully whether appropriate steps have been taken to maintain such confidentiality. Email is not inherently a more secure medium of communication than traditional means, and emails can be easily copied, forwarded and stored.

Security

Do not give internal passwords to anyone outside the company. In addition, you must not give any customer-related security information to anyone other than the customer unless specifically authorized in writing by the customer in advance.

Records

Keep proper records of our dealings with outsiders. It is always possible that what appears to be a relatively trivial point could be of immense significance later. It is not possible to foresee what will subsequently need to be checked so keep a complete record of all transactions.

Data protection

If you have access to data about individuals you must bear in mind at all times the provisions of the Data Protection Act 1998. Guidance on these may be obtained from the HR Department.

Passwords

Use passwords at all times and change them at the intervals notified to you. Do not select obvious passwords. All passwords must be kept confidential.

Backups

Regular backups must be carried out in accordance with the rules laid down from time to time. Critical information should not be stored on the hard disk of your workstation in case it is lost.

Misuse

Misuse of computers is a serious disciplinary offence. The following are examples of misuse:

- fraud and theft;
- system sabotage;
- introducing viruses and time bombs;
- using unauthorized software;
- obtaining unauthorized access;
- using the system for unauthorized private work or game playing;
- breaches of the Data Protection Act 1998;
- sending abusive, rude or defamatory messages via email;
- hacking;
- breach of the company's security procedures or this policy.

This list is not exhaustive. Depending on the circumstances of each case, misuse of the computer system may be considered gross misconduct, punishable by dismissal without notice. Misuse amounting to criminal conduct may be reported by us to the police.

Breaches

All breaches of computer security must be referred to the IT Department. If you suspect that a fellow employee (of whatever seniority) is abusing the computer system you may speak in confidence to the HR Department. You are responsible for any actions that are taken against us by a third party arising from restricted and/or offensive material being displayed on, or sent by you through, our computer system.

Monitoring

The company reserves the right to intercept and monitor your communications, including email, internet and telephone calls. This right to monitor may be exercised, for example, to decide whether communications are relevant to the business, to prevent or detect crime and to ensure the effective operation of the system. In addition, the company reserves the right to monitor communications in order to determine the existence of facts, to detect unauthorized use of the system and to decide the standards which ought to be achieved by employees using the system.

Improvements

We welcome suggestions from you for the improvement of this policy. These should be directed to the HR Department.

5 Instructing an IT Consultant

JEAN MORGAN

This chapter outlines the points that you should consider when employing an IT consultant. The appendix gives a template for a terms of reference document.

INTRODUCTION

In recent years, the use of consultants has made headlines. John Prescott was accused of wasting millions of pounds on consultants when he led the huge Department of the Environment, Transport and the Regions. The falling profits and share price of Marks & Spencer led to an influx of consultants. The BBC took much criticism for its well-publicized use of consultants under John Birt's leadership. Under Greg Dyke, a source is reported to have said, 'The age of croissants and consultants is over.' (Arlidge 2002) Bob Townsend famously referred to the consultants who 'borrow the client's watch, tell him the time, and pocket the watch with the fee.' (Lambert 1997)

But consultants are not all bad. Few organizations have an experienced management team with all of the expertise it requires both to run existing operations and to take risks in new growth areas. The advantage of buying in consultancy support is to blend detailed in-house knowledge with fresh and objective sources of information. With the right approach, this can be achieved.

SO YOU THINK YOU NEED A CONSULTANT?

There are many reasons why an organization will look outside for additional resource. It may be that the resource requirement is for additional people or it may be for additional knowledge. Consultants can meet the demands of either requirement but the client must know which type of resource is required.

If your organization is embarking on something that it does not do often and if that something has IT implications, then you would look to a consultant to bring knowledge of that area into your business. It may be that you're looking to develop into a new business area with a new product or service offering, or you're trying to enter new markets, or you're re-locating or facing legislative or regulatory change. Or you may feel that your IT group has become stale when your requests are turned down with excuses like 'Our infrastructure doesn't cope with that' or 'But we've always done it that way' or 'That's the way things are done around here'. That's a demand for additional knowledge, which may be new to the organization or even new to all organizations. The latter was, of course, the case, when the ecommerce channel developed at such a fast pace a couple of years ago and everyone had to have an ebusiness.

On the other hand, your team may know what needs to be done but need more people to do it in acceptable time. This makes the selection process easier because you'll have a better understanding of the skills required. You may also be looking to consultants because there isn't time to recruit a permanent member of staff, so it could be an interim position. Sometimes, budgetary situations mean that it is easier to bring in a consultant than to increase a department's permanent head count; ours is not to reason why the accountants work this way... Either way, the consultant market is waiting to fulfil your request.

FINDING A CONSULTANT

It is important to keep in mind that the search for consultancy support is a procurement exercise and not a personnel recruitment or employment exercise. Both result in finding people to do work but there are important differences. We will exclude any further consideration of permanent recruitment. So let us consider where you will find the most suitable consultant for your needs. There is a range of different sources.

Agencies

Recruitment and Human Resources agencies are sometimes called body shops. A good agency will help to shape the requirement through thorough knowledge of the industry, and will do some sifting of responses. A poor agency will add little value and bombard you with a quantity of applicants rather than quality. Consultants are not employed by the agency: each consultant is likely to be self-employed or part of small limited company. Consultants will often call themselves, or be referred to as, contractors. There are tens of thousands of such consultants.

While good agencies can be relied on to build up a relationship with freelance consultants and may provide a quality assurance service on the consultant's work, they are unfortunately in the minority and many agencies have no idea of the consultant's methods and approach. If a replacement is required to take over from a consultant in the event of sickness or non-performance, then the new one may have quite different methods of working. Market forces will tend to root out the bad agencies because clients won't retain them once they find them out, and you would be unlikely to find long or repeat assignments on the CV. Agencies tend to be used for one-off requirements and for small numbers of individuals. They are able to respond very quickly to a requirement and have access to a huge pool of individuals at all skill levels. The better and longer-established large agencies sometimes try to work in the same way as systems integrators and management consultancies.

Systems integrators

Systems integrators (SI) are sometimes still known as software houses; the terms are synonymous. A 'software house' is a firm that writes bespoke software for clients or develops packaged software. The newer name, 'systems integrator', reflects the reducing practice of building systems from new program code and is more about putting together components or adding new systems to your existing software.

Companies such as LogicaCMG and IBM Global Services fall into this category. Consultants are likely to be full-time permanent employees of the systems integrator although, when demand is high, systems integrators also use self-employed independent consultants (called 'associates'). The consultant supplied by an SI is expected to conform to the company culture, methods and quality standards of the integrator. The company would be expected to provide alternative people should the consultant be unable to complete the work. An SI tends to supply a team of people to solve a requirement and it may put the entire team together as a package deal; the client may have limited influence, in practice, over the composition of the team. The SI may have a vested interest in supplying a solution from one of their business partners, though this should be disclosed to you. The SI is likely to be more expensive than an agency solution; margins need to be higher to cover the overheads of employing consultants full-time when demands vary over time.

Management consultancies

Very similar to a systems integrator, a management consultancy is likely to be more expensive. A management consultancy tends to be used for strategic business projects and would bring in IT specialists as required. Examples of management consultancies are Accenture, AMTEC Consulting plc, Bourton Group Limited, Cap Gemini Ernst & Young, Computer Sciences Corporation (CSC), Deloitte Consulting, HEDRA Limited, and PA Consulting Group, amongst many others.

The Institute of Management Consultancy (IMC) promotes excellence in management consultancy. Its website, at www.imc.co.uk, offers the facility to search for consultants in specialisms such as information technology and ebusiness, the internet, and project management. All registered practices must meet certain minimum standards set by the Institute. For instance, at least 51% of the principals of a practice must be a Certified Management Consultant and the practice must conform to the IMC Code of Conduct.

The Management Consultancies Association (MCA) website is at www.mca.org.uk. It represents the leading management consulting firms in the UK, which currently employ over 20000 consultants and generate near-ly £4 billion in annual fee income. It will help to select a consulting firm for a potential client. One of the main objectives of the MCA is to maintain high standards within the UK management consultancy industry by ensuring that member firms meet its stringent entry criteria and adhere to its code of conduct. An equally important role for the MCA is to ensure that users of consultancy are aware of its standards and that they adopt best practice in their dealings with management consultancy firms.

Academia

A source of consultancy which is often overlooked is the local University or College. For work in new technologies, the academic world can be a useful one. However, the bureaucracy that the potential client has to navigate before finding a department which may source the requirement can often be a barrier. At the practitioner level, student placements are often very successful and provide benefits to both client and student consultant. Mature students, in particular, can bring the benefits of prior business experience.

The supervisory requirements of an educational establishment are usual-ly less onerous than may initially seem the case. In one project to imple-ment a new accounting system, the project manager chanced upon an information systems student who had previously worked in a finance department. The value of his contribution to the project far exceeded his cost since his knowledge of accounting was a great asset.

The British Computer Society

Worklink

The British Computer Society (BCS) Young Professionals Group has set up a service called Worklink, at www.worklink.org.uk. This aims to help stu-dents find placements with companies during a gap or sandwich year. Employers can register and search the database of CVs online. The database contains only the details of BCS members.

Professional advice register

In addition to the student service, the BCS maintains a register of members who can provide advice as a consultant, a security specialist or an expert witness. The purpose of the register is to enable users and managers to con-tact a pool of qualified professionals with established competence and integrity. There are three components to the register:

- Consultancy: registrants are professional members of the Society.
- Security Specialists: the experience of the registrants has been tested by peer interviews. This is open to non-BCS members provided they accept the same terms and conditions as members.
- Expert Witness: registrants are corporate members of the Society and

belong at an appropriate grade to one of four accredited professional bodies concerned with legal aspects of expert witness work.

All registrants are bound by the Society's Code of Conduct and appropriate Codes of Practice, breaches of which are subject to disciplinary procedures. Registrants have at least six years experience in information systems.

The register can be found at www.bcs.org under the Products & Services tab.

The internet

Many independent, freelance consultants now have their own websites, reachable via search engines or portals. These consultants can be good value because there are no intermediary fees and lower overheads. An independent consultant may belong to a small network of trusted associates. There is often no formal business relationship between the consultants but rather a practical network based on experience of working together, trust and referrals. This model is similar to Charles Handy's portfolio workers (1994). You can find these consultants through search engines or word of mouth.

The golf course

Complementing the formal channels, word of mouth recommendation is a powerful source. So the golf course, or anywhere else where you network and meet people whose advice you trust, is an opportunity to take a referral. There are benefits, such as timesaving and, again, no intermediary fees, but it is critical to make sure that the type of work covers similar areas of competence, e.g. a web site designer may have a very different skill set from a web services integrator.

SELECTING THE RIGHT CONSULTANT

Some element of due diligence is essential to ensure that the intermediary is a good supplier and that the consultant's track record is authentic. Aim to see evidence of any claims that the supplier makes. For example, take up client references and seek evidence of any claimed track record. Most organizations have a process for evaluating new suppliers, considering company background, financial status, client references and so on. Many now operate a 'Preferred Supplier' list for some or all of the sources of consultants, which reduces the need for examination of the suppliers on the list and should reduce the lead time and costs of procurement; there may be a call-off arrangement or framework agreement. Whatever process you use, consider the burden that the examination may put on the supplier and make it appropriate to the size of the reward for success and the likelihood of success.

If you are running a competition among suppliers, be open about the scale of the competition. Although confidentiality is important, for example in safeguarding CVs and fee rates, you should aim to be as open as practical with the suppliers. This enables the suppliers to gauge how much effort to spend on the response. The end result should be transparent so that the reasons for rejection and acceptance are obvious. Then the relationship stands a better chance of remaining positive and there is healthier basis for any future opportunities. Many intermediaries have started to use the word 'partnership' for the potential commercial relationship; be wary of the temptation to think that the supplier is offering anything special, though, unless there is true sharing of risk and reward. Due diligence on the supplier and the consultant may include minimum levels of Professional Indemnity insurance, accreditation to or membership of professional institutes, and evidence of qualifications. But be clear in your own mind whether these requirements are really essential or are 'nice to have'. You will potentially exclude some excellent people if the hurdles are set unnecessarily high.

PRICING STRUCTURES

Commercial practices are addressed in Chapter 2. Be aware, especially in a supplier's market, that some of the big systems integrators, agencies and management consultants can be pretty inflexible in their contract terms and conditions.

The question of whether to engage consulting services on a time and materials or a fixed price basis can be answered only with full knowledge of the client's requirements, the supplier background, and the business environment. Bear in mind the market conditions, and commit only for what you know needs doing. By building a strong relationship with the supplier, it is often possible to make a soft commitment for work beyond the contractual commitment, although there is a risk that the consultant will line up other work beyond the formal commitment to you. This has to be offset against the financial commitment that you are prepared to make. The relationship should be open enough for the consultant to discuss this with you should the need arise, and the ethos of the 'gentleman's agreement' does still exist.

A fixed price arrangement is often appealing but can cause much more initial work for the client. While there may be interim payments, to ease the supplier's cash flow, the client will only pay in full when the consultant has achieved a pre-defined deliverable. This means that the client must ensure that the deliverable specification is absolutely what he expects, wants or needs. The client should then need to exercise little day to day control over the consultant. The consultant's motivation and risk may be maximized, but it is important that the client also finds a way to manage his own risk should the consultant not actually deliver.

The time and materials approach can be appropriate if the end result is not defined in detail and if the client will exert management control during delivery. The consultant carries less risk but will want to ensure that there is some notice of termination, so he is not left high and dry with no work in the pipeline. A time and materials approach is often used for a short piece of work to specify a project or deliverables that can then be delivered subsequently under a fixed price approach.

There are also fixed duration arrangements where a consultant may be engaged for a set number of days or months at a fixed daily rate. These tend to be used where a consultant is needed to augment the in-house head count.

The Dynamic Systems Development Method (DSDM) Consortium has drafted an outline contract for Rapid Application Development projects where consultants may be used. This contains some elements of fixed price work and some work that sounds like an open-ended service contract. The use is licensed like open source code and feedback is requested on its use in real situations.

ASSESSING SKILLS AND KNOWLEDGE

Remember the important questions when selecting people: 'Has he done it? Can he do it? Will he do it?' Does the consultant have the actual experience you are after? Does he have relevant similar experience which means he could quickly learn the new skills and apply them correctly to the requirement? And does he have the right attitude to fit in?

However, you should also remember that Christopher Columbus would never have set sail if he had waited for people with experience of discovering new worlds; there were no candidates with experience of landing on the moon when President Kennedy recruited for the space race. Actual experience in a particular area may be genuinely thin on the ground or even non-existent in the quantities you require, particularly if this is a new technology or business area. Often, the true need is that the consultant has the right aptitude. Many people have seen very quick and successful skills acquisition, provided the consultant possesses the right qualities.

The third question is at least as important as the other two. Meredith Belbin (1996) described nine team roles: the Plant, the Resource Investigator, the Co-ordinator, the Shaper, the Monitor Evaluator, the Teamworker, the Implementer, the Completer and the Specialist. To work most effectively, a team requires these roles and it will be sub-optimal if any one is lacking.

You should draft terms of reference for the selection exercise using the template in the Appendix as a basis. You may not be able to complete all of the headings or to provide full detail. It is, however, extremely beneficial to work through the terms of reference, as it focuses the requirement and helps to ensure that all the implications of the work have been considered. It is usual to formally agree the Terms of Reference document with the consultant only after the consultant has had some time for orientation into the assignment.

GETTING VALUE FROM THE CONSULTANT

A well-written Terms of Reference document will improve the chances of achieving a good result from the use of consultancy services, and the successful use of a consultant will result in a win–win situation. The client organization can win because it has better knowledge than before and it will have made progress in an area which wouldn't have been possible without the consultant's help. A good consultant can leave the client's permanent staff motivated if they have learnt new skills, have taken on improved ways of working or better processes, and if they have been part of a successful piece of work. The consultant wins if he walks away with his reputation enhanced, the possibility of a new client reference, and with the door open for future opportunities for re-engagement.

Some clients try to schedule a handover or skills transfer from the consultant at the end of an assignment; this is very challenging and is often compressed to fit a shortened timescale. We have all spent time doing documentation to hand over to those left with a piece of work. There is a tendency to document the easy bits because they're easiest to document and spend less time on the difficult bits. Bear in mind what Confucius said, 'I hear and I forget. I see and I remember. I do and I understand.' If the handover is all at the end of an assignment, where is the opportunity for the 'doing'? The client and consultant should work together positively to create situations for learning.

> Sharing knowledge is not about giving people something, or getting something from them. That is only valid for information sharing. Sharing knowledge occurs when people are genuinely interested in helping one another develop new capacities for action; it is about creating learning processes. (Senge 1990)

In other words, knowledge transfer is not something to fit into the last few days of an assignment.

WHEN ALL ELSE FAILS

A poorly-written Terms of Reference document significantly increases the likelihood that the consultancy experience will fail. The consultant may, deliberately or innocently, misinterpret unclear terms of reference to his advantage. From the client's side, he is left with little or no protection because sloppy objectives and deliverables will mean that acceptance will be ambiguous. This is how disputes may arise.

If you run into difficulties with the execution of a consultancy assignment, then the BCS, the IMC and the MCA all have a disciplinary procedure for breaches of their respective codes. Mediation has a good track record in resolving disputes, while litigation is a last resort.

While we all work at making best use of consultant resources in our organizations, take some solace from Tom Lambert (1997, page 2). He admitted, in misquoting Churchill, that the buyer of consultancy services 'is investing in something which is in the nature of a mystery wrapped in an enigma'. Need we say more?

APPENDIX: TEMPLATE FOR A TERMS OF REFERENCE DOCUMENT

The Terms of Reference document should provide a clear, unambiguous description of the work. It helps to avoid misunderstandings and mismatched expectations. In general, you may provide less detail for roles with less responsibility. Some standard headings are described below.

Background

Why the work needs doing: summarize the business case for the work and what's been done or looked at so far.

Objectives

The goals may be soft, but there should be some measurable objectives e.g. implement the new payroll system by the end of the calendar year so that 90% of all employees are paid correctly and on time through the new system.

Scope

Refer both to what's in and what's out of scope e.g. the Payroll system is in scope; the accounting system and interfaces to the accounting system will not change and are out of scope.

Constraints

List any limits on the resources that the consultant may use, such as financial budget and staff time usage. Specify any standards with which the consultant must comply e.g. quality management system, TickIT processes, development methods (such as RAD, DSDM or SSADM), project management standards (such as PRINCE2), progress reporting standards.

Assumptions

It is quite tricky to write down the issues that are 'taken as read'. In an implementation project, the assumptions would include that the previous project to select the software had chosen the right package. Then if the software package turns out to be a problem, the consultant can not be criticized for that aspect of his work.

In 2000, a financial services company undertook an assessment of the work they would have to do if the UK were to join EMU. For that exercise, which used consultants in some roles, there was an assumption that demand for euro-based products would start low but would increase sharply. This assumption had a big effect on the designs for potential new products.

Resources

List the resources which the consultant may use. This includes the consultant's budget for his/her time and whether full-time or part-time availability is expected. There are advantages to part-time assignments: they can help to maintain the consultant's objectivity, can prevent the risk of the consultant 'going native' and can work out less expensive. Consider whether travel to off-site facilities is expected and how expenses are reimbursed.

Resource considerations should include office facilities, desk, storage space, desktop computer, network access for email and document access, telephone usage. The consultant may manage permanent staff or other consultants: this must be specified.

If you, as the client, provide some resources, give some thought to what happens when your supply of that resource fails. For example, in one testing assignment, the mainframe failed and continued to be unreliable for over a week, and a team of half a dozen consultants could not carry out the tests. Some of the self-employed consultants took (unpaid) holiday. A couple of consultants from a systems integration company went back and were not charged to that client. But the remainder continued to charge the client, as the inability to do fully productive work was outside their control.

Bear in mind, too, that if the consultant uses his/her own equipment, then irritating issues can arise over such seemingly trivial issues like which versions of Microsoft products to use and the risk of importing a virus.

Reporting

Who does the consultant report to, how often, and in what format?

Responsibilities and Roles

Who are the stakeholders and what is their relationship with the consultant? Think about all of the people who have a stake in the success or failure of the work. For example, explain who is the sponsor of the work (i.e. who will pick up the bill) and identify who is the day to day administrative and support contact for the consultant.

Deliverables

A key definition of what is expected from the consultant. Make sure it is clear who owns the deliverable at the end of the assignment so that intellectual property rights issues do not arise.

Acceptance

State how you and the consultant will know that the assignment deliverables are complete. Think carefully about this and be as precise as possible.

Good acceptance criteria are objective, verifiable and realistic. This is key should disputes arise. It is also worth considering an escalation route should disagreements arise about whether the criteria have been met. Each deliverable may have different acceptance criteria and may be accepted by a different client representative.

Issues

List here any relevant issues which remain to be resolved. It is not the consultant's responsibility to resolve them, otherwise they would be listed in the Deliverables section, but they may impinge on the deliverables.

Interfaces

Specify any teams, departments or suppliers that the consultant may have to contact. Also list any technical interfaces which need to be taken into account in the work.

REFERENCES

Arlidge, J. (2002) 'Dyke's new mantra for the future BBC: Only connect'. *The Observer,* 6 January 2002. Available at http://media.guardian.co.uk/broadcast/story/0,7493,628509,00.html.

Belbin, M. (1996) *Team Roles at Work.* Oxford: Heinemann.

Handy, C. (1994) *The Empty Raincoat: Making sense of the future.* London: Hutchinson.

Lambert, T. (1997) *High Income Consulting: How to build and market your professional practice.* Yarmouth, ME: Nicholas Brealey.

Senge, P. (1990) *The Fifth Discipline: Art and practice of the learning organization.* Doubleday. Quoted at http://www.gurteen.com.

6 Intellectual Property Law for Computer Users

JENNIFER PIERCE

Intellectual property law is a relatively complex subject. This chapter concentrates on the more important aspects for users, so that you are aware of the pitfalls and know when to seek professional advice. The appendix provides a basic guide to intellectual property and explains the terminology in use.

INTRODUCTION

Intellectual property is an inescapable element of modern business, especially in the field of information technology. It protects both suppliers' rights in the systems that they provide and users' rights in aspects of their usage. Everybody needs to know roughly who owns each part of a computer system and how that impacts on its use. They also need to know what not to do with the equipment on the internet, so as to avoid being sued.

There are five main types of intellectual property in the UK:

- Patents – protect inventions, which could be found in any part of a computer system. Software as such is not technically patentable, but if it has other features that fulfil the criteria for patentability this will not prevent the grant of a patent.

- Design – there are, technically, four different types of right, which also overlap with copyright. They cover items that are as diverse as semi-conductors and computer graphics.

- Copyright – protects literary, artistic and other works. Software is a literary work and graphical user interfaces are artistic works.

- Database right – covers collections of data that are accessible by electronic or other means.

- Trade marks – broadly, protect brands, such as 'Microsoft' and 'Intel'.

For those who are not familiar with intellectual property, at the end of the chapter there is a further explanation of these rights. Rights in other territories, even European Union (EU) territories, may be different, although some rights are harmonized throughout the EU.

HARDWARE AND INTELLECTUAL PROPERTY RIGHTS

Hardware is a bit of a misnomer, as much hardware contains systems software too. From an intellectual property perspective, the distinction is very important, as the real hardware element is sold but the systems software is usually licensed (see the next section), although there is a current legal debate over whether this is appropriate. If hardware is protected this is generally by patents and/or designs, although brands are extremely important in this sector.

The non-software element is treated like any other gadget. If it is protected, you need authority from the person who owns the intellectual property to manufacture, sell, or import it and so on. However, after the first authorized sale of the hardware in the European Economic Area (EEA), all those rights are 'exhausted' in the EEA, unless there are special conditions on the sale. This means that if the equipment comes from an authorized source you can do what you like with it, unless there is a special arrangement or you export it from the EEA or do drastic repairs that amount to remaking it (or bits of it).

Authorized sales

So everything is fine if you buy from an authorized source, but how do you tell who is authorized and who is not? There are plenty of people who call themselves 'authorized dealers'. Some will be fully authorized under all of the necessary rights, some will have limited rights, and others may not be authorized at all.

You can always check the status of a dealer with the equipment manufacturer. Unfortunately, even reputable dealers appointed by equipment manufacturers may not have all the necessary rights, as it can be very difficult to check who has relevant rights.

The reason for this is that registered intellectual property, such as patents, gives the owner a monopoly. This means, broadly, that anybody making and selling equipment within the specification of some intellectual property without permission can be infringing that property, even if they are unaware that the rights exist.

Currently, the amount of registered intellectual property is increasing rapidly, so it can be difficult to search for it. This means that even the larger computer manufacturers may sell infringing hardware without knowing about it, although this is less likely, as they have considerable facilities for searching.

Technically, the owner of intellectual property can seize infringing equipment, so it is a serious matter. However, in practice it is rare for an intellectual property owner to seize equipment from end users.

So what should you do? There should be a relatively low risk if you buy hardware from a reputable supplier who gives you a full indemnity (see Chapter 2, page 22, intellectual property rights) to cover the situation where the hardware infringes somebody else's intellectual property. You should also pick a supplier with a 'deep pocket', which will be sure to meet its obligations under the indemnity.

Special conditions

Some intellectual property owners attach special conditions to the sale of their equipment. This is not the technical terminology, but is an easy way of describing what happens. For example, they may insist that you do not take it outside a particular territory or that you only use it with another piece of equipment. Some of these conditions are unenforceable as they breach trade laws, but others may be enforceable. Most restrictions on exporting goods that have been brought in one EEA country to another EEA country are unenforceable.

Repairs

When you have bought equipment you generally have a right to repair it, although repairs by somebody who is not authorized by the manufacturer may affect your guarantee (see Chapter 2, page 23, suppliers warranties). If the repair entails replacing parts that are covered by intellectual property, the same rules apply to repairs as applied to the original sale, so this sort of repair must be made by an authorized person.

SOFTWARE AND INTELLECTUAL PROPERTY RIGHTS

Copying and adapting – the general rules

Copyright is the main form of intellectual property protecting software so it is treated differently from hardware. Software can also be protected by some of the rights protecting hardware, including registered rights. So all of the rules relating to hardware may apply, but there are additional things to think about.

Copyright protects against copying, adapting and distributing copies of the protected material to the public. It can protect against other things, but these are the main types of protection in this context. You cannot copy, adapt or distribute copies of software to the public unless you own the copyright or have the authorization ('licence') of the copyright owner.

It is fairly unusual for a user to own copyright, as most software houses want to grant licences to several users in order to reduce costs and to make maintenance both cheaper and more profitable. However, if a supplier is making a bespoke program and you are to pay the full economic costs of this, there are strong arguments that you should own the copyright if the program is stand alone. If you are to own the copyright you need a document that transfers the rights to you.

Simply running software involves copying it, so if you do not own the rights you need a licence to run it. You also need a licence if you are going to alter it, because that amounts to adaptation. In practice, few software houses will simply allow you to copy and adapt their software. They tend to specify precisely what you can do with it.

You also need a licence if you are going to rent, lend or broadcast copyright material. As the average software user does not want to do any of these things, they are not covered in this book.

Backup copies

Whatever the licence says, there are some things that the supplier cannot stop you from doing. So if you have a licence, the supplier cannot stop you from making backup copies if you need them for your permitted use of the software.

Maintenance

As a general rule, you can copy or adapt software if that is necessary for you to use the software, provided that the licence doesn't stop you. So, for example, you can adapt software to correct errors, unless the licence specifically says that you cannot do it.

Decompilation and interfaces

You can decompile a program if you want to create an interface with another program, provided that you do not use the information that you glean from this to do anything else and do not give it to anybody who does not need it to build the interface. Similarly, if you can get the information from another source (such as the supplier) or if you use it to build a copycat program, the decompilation is not permitted.

What does all this mean in practice?

In many cases, it is just not feasible to change the printed terms that you will be offered. The terms may not be enforceable if they are unreasonable, but that is a hard call for you to make without advice and you should never depend on it.

Have a good look at the scope of the licence and look for anything that you would want to do that is left out. If it says 'copy and adapt' you will have no problems, unless you want to sell copies, and most suppliers only allow professional distributors to do that. If it is of more limited scope and sets out a list of things that you can do, you need to scrutinize the list.

Many users cannot and do not want to maintain software. But they may want to know that they can go to another supplier if something goes wrong. This is precisely what many suppliers want to avoid, as they do not want anybody else meddling with their trade secrets, or depriving them of maintenance fees. So some clients ask for maintenance rights, whilst many suppliers try to avoid granting them; in the end, it is a matter for discussion, although the supplier will often win the argument.[1]

You will encounter similar problems with decompilation, but in that case the supplier can only prohibit decompilation if it provides sufficient information to allow you to build an interface. So this is less of a problem.

---

[1] In any event, the right to adapt for the purpose of maintenance may well be of limited use unless you have a copy of the source code. This topic is dealt with in more detail in Chapter 7.

Transferring a licence

Many licences prohibit the transfer of rights to somebody else and some-times the consent of the licensor is required before the rights can be trans-ferred. So this may limit the scope for selling on systems. Before you sell or transfer a computer, you need to check that you can pass on rights in the software and possibly rights under maintenance contracts, depending on the circumstances. This can be crucial in the context of outsourcing.

Non-compliance

Needless to say, if you do something outside the scope of your licence, which is prohibited by copyright, technically you are infringing copyright and the copyright owner may sue you and seize the software. In practice, if you do something accidentally and no real harm is done, the copyright owner may give you a warning, without taking the matter any further.

DATABASES AND INTELLECTUAL PROPERTY RIGHTS

Taking a licence on somebody else's rights

The intellectual property rights protecting databases are relatively easy to understand provided that you can envisage the constituent parts of a data-base. Databases are usually manipulated by software. Then there is the form of the actual database, the collection of data to populate it, and final-ly individual items of data.

From a legal perspective, the software is no different from any other soft-ware. The form of the database is protected by copyright in a similar way to software. The collection of data may be protected by copyright, but only to a limited degree. A far more useful right in this context is database right, which protects the contents of the database against substantial extraction and re-utilization. Individual items of data, such as photographs, may also be protected by copyright.

So what does this add up to, in practice? It means that you need a licence to use any of the rights protecting a database that you do not own. You need to ensure that the licence covers the way that you envisage using the data-base in terms of extraction and re-utilization of data. In particular, if you are using a database to extract large amounts of data, you need to watch out for any limits on usage.

Protecting your own rights

It also means that in setting up your database and populating it you will acquire rights in the data that you assemble provided that you or your employees do this, or you acquire the rights under a written contract with the person who does.

If you ever need to enforce your rights you will need to prove that they are still current. This entails keeping records of the dates when the database is finished, or made available to the public (if earlier), together with a copy of the database at that time. You need to do the same thing each time that it is substantially updated, as major updates may qualify for further protection.

You also need records of the nationality of the person, company or partnership that took the financial risks of making it. The database will only qualify for protection if the maker is from the EEA. If it is a company it must be incorporated in the EEA with either its central administration or principal place of business in the EEA or its registered office and a firm base in the EEA.

It is worthwhile marking all copies of the database with the name of the owner. This may deter infringers and will help you to claim damages from them. It could also, potentially, be used as evidence of the origin of any pirate copies.

WEBSITES AND INTELLECTUAL PROPERTY RIGHTS

Make sure that you own your website

Many people spend a great deal of money on websites, but allow the designer to own rights in them. It is a bit like buying something and leaving part of it in the shop on a permanent basis. Nonetheless, appreciable numbers of people do this, probably because they are now used to somebody else owning the software that they use.

The contents of a website are protected by copyright, which arises automatically when it is created, provided that it is first published in the UK (or another country, such as an EU state that is party to the same treaty as the UK) or fulfils certain other criteria. It is also possible to apply for registered designs in respect of specific graphics such as icons. As this is a registered right, it gives monopoly protection, which means that anybody else using a design within the scope of the registration will infringe.

Trade mark protection may be available for signs that are used on your website. These can overlap with registered designs in this context. As a very general rule, in the UK, trade mark applications are more expensive to process than ones for designs. However, trade marks can give broader protection and they can last indefinitely if you pay the renewal fees.

Many websites are dependent on software to assist in navigation and to process data that is input. The same rules apply to this software as to any other software. Similarly, there may be a facility for accessing and searching a database and that database should be treated in the same way as any other database.

Look after your rights

Copyright, registered designs and trade marks can all be valuable assets of a business, and can be used to protect it against imitators, so you should aim to own rights in your website. Consultants who build websites are likely to use certain generic material on each job. They would be foolish to give this to you, but anything that is specific to your project should be yours and you should protect it.

Before your designer starts work, you should have a written agreement, transferring rights in the material he creates to you and obliging the designer to keep the designs confidential in case you want to register them. Otherwise, the designer may be able to argue that he owns the copyright, and you just have a licence or somebody else may try to register the design before you do.

If you own the copyright in your website, it is worthwhile marking it to deter infringers, to ensure that you can claim damages from them and to take advantage of protection under international copyright treaties. You should put the © symbol followed by the name of the copyright owner and the date of first publication on the website.

If you put material onto a website, visitors are entitled to assume that they can use it in some way, so you need to be clear about what they can do. For example, if they can make copies solely for domestic use, but not for a business or any other purpose, you must state that specifically. Similarly, if they may not adapt it or give other people copies, you need to say so and the notices must be prominent so that they cannot miss them.

It is easy to catch infringers on the web

The second thing to remember about websites is that they are very public. Some people think that infringement of intellectual property goes unnoticed on the web. The truth is that sophisticated software has been developed to search for infringers, especially trade mark infringers. It is also easier to prove infringement as the evidence is recorded. See the sections below on internet use for further information on infringement.

DOMAIN NAMES AND INTELLECTUAL PROPERTY RIGHTS

Why there are problems

In the 1990s one of the more memorable rackets was buying up domain names that corresponded to famous trade marks and then holding the trade mark owner to ransom by demanding vast sums to transfer the domain name to them. Courts in many jurisdictions have now put a stop to this by holding that the 'cyber-squatters' are infringing trade marks.

Unfortunately, that is not the end of the story, as there are still problems with domain names and trade marks. Trade marks are registrable in 45 different classes of goods and services and it is possible to sub-divide each class by specifying only some of the goods or services within that class. So a great many businesses with the same trade mark may co-exist without problems.

This is not so with domain names, as it is only possible to register a name once. So, for example, if the BCS has registered 'BCS.org' nobody else can register 'BCS' with the top level domain of '.org'. The situation has improved with the creation of further top level domains, such as '.biz', but the old ones like '.com' are still the most popular.

Opposing a registration

Domain names are generally allocated to the first person to register, although there were special arrangements for trade mark owners to have priority when the last set of top level domains were first allocated. This means that if somebody has already registered the name that you are seeking to register, you will only be able to oppose the registration in limited circumstances.

You can complain if a name within the top level domains, such as '.com', '.net', or '.org':

- is identical or confusingly similar to your trade mark; and
- the person using the domain name has no right or legitimate interest in that domain name; and
- the person using the domain name registered it and is using it in bad faith.

The domain name registry may cancel the domain name or transfer it. In some circumstances it is unclear whether there has been bad faith but in others, such as cyber-squatting, this has been relatively easy to decide. This also applies to certain country-code top level domains. In the case of other top level domains, the grounds for opposition will depend on the rules of the domain name registry concerned.

In addition to using the procedure in the relevant domain name registry, it is also possible to bring an action for trade mark infringement in a conventional court, although this may be difficult if the domain name owner is in a different business and the trade mark is not well known. In the US, anti-cyber-squatting legislation may be of use.

Avoiding disputes

If a domain name is not used, or is not commercially important, and where there are no grounds for opposing its continued registration, it may be possible to purchase the domain name for a relatively modest sum.

In practice the best way to avoid disputes is to register a domain name early and, if you can afford it, registering a corresponding trade mark in the same jurisdiction as the domain name registry can help too. If you think that there are grounds for opposing a domain name registration, it is best to seek professional advice.

It goes without saying, that if you are registering a domain name, you need to be careful to avoid infringing somebody else's trade mark (see the next section).

THE INTERNET AND TRADE MARKS

Infringement

The international trade mark system has historically been divided by national boundaries or by trading blocks. Internet use is international by its very nature, so if you use a trade mark on the internet there is a technical possibility of infringing separate trade marks in a large number of territories. Registration in one or more jurisdictions will not protect you from infringement in others.

In order to infringe a trade mark, it is usually necessary to use a similar mark for the same or similar goods or services as the trade mark is registered for. In Europe, if the mark or services are similar but not identical, and you want to claim infringement you must show that people would be confused about where the goods or services come from.

Well-known marks are a special case, as it is possible to infringe them by trading in different goods or services and in the EU (including the UK) if without due cause the use would take unfair advantage of the mark or be detrimental to it. In the US, use of marks that blurs their distinctiveness or tarnishes their reputation may also amount to trade mark dilution.

Some uses, such as referring to the owner's goods and services in an honest way, will not infringe in some territories.

In practice, it is most likely that somebody will take action if you are actively using a mark in a particular jurisdiction, more especially if you trade there or have assets in that jurisdiction, as the trade mark owner then has a more realistic possibility of suing you successfully.

What should you do?

There is no easy answer to this, as laws and trading methods are still being developed. Full international searches are prohibitively expensive for many companies. However, it should be possible to search for trade marks in the major jurisdictions before using a mark on the internet. If you cannot afford a professional search by a trade mark attorney, some patent offices, such as the UK, provide limited internet searching facilities. Nonetheless, a professional search is always preferable.

Examples of infringement

In addition to using a trade mark on a website, or as a domain name, the most likely ways in which trade marks can be infringed on the internet are through:

Linking and framing

There are two types of links on web pages: hypertext links and inline links. With a hypertext link, you click on an icon and your browser retrieves material from a second website. With an inline link, material from a second website is automatically retrieved by and shows as an integral part of the first website.

Framing is an extreme form of linking where material from the linked site is framed by advertising and other material from the first site, so that it appears as if it is all on the same site. Linking technologies allow people to pretend that somebody else's content is theirs. Links that bypass the home page of another site can bypass valuable advertising.

In terms of intellectual property, linking can lead to confusion over whose products are being displayed under which marks. So, for example, the marks from the linked site may appear with products from the first site and the products of the linked site may appear under the trade marks of the first site.

Legally this may amount to trade mark infringement, unfair competition or passing off, depending on the jurisdiction, so it is safest not to skip home pages and to inform users that they are entering another site.

Metatags

Search engines find and classify websites by reference to keywords. Website owners assist the engines by embedding keywords, to increase use of their sites. Some unscrupulous people have embedded competitors' trade marks and well known marks as keywords to try to divert business to their sites. In the UK, this usually amounts to trade mark infringement and, in the case of competitors, to passing off. There are similar remedies available in other jurisdictions.

Keyword advertising, where banner advertisements are linked to keyword search terms, presents similar problems, although in many cases generic words will be used so there will be no trade mark infringement or passing off.

THE INTERNET AND COPYRIGHT

Publishing literature, art and music on the internet, as well as other forms of broadcasting, merit a separate book, so they are not included in this chapter. Basic copying from websites is dealt with in the section on websites. The aspect of ordinary usage that merits further mention is the copyright aspect of linking, which is described in the trade mark section above.

Creating links does not infringe copyright, as the material on the other website is not copied or otherwise affected when the link is created.

APPENDIX: A BASIC GUIDE TO INTELLECTUAL PROPERTY AND RELATED RIGHTS

Copyright

What is copyright?

Copyright protects the means of expression of concepts, including literary works, fine art, crafts, music, films, broadcasts, and so on. In order to qualify, works must be original; that is to say that they have not been copied, although there is a different test for databases (see section below). There is usually a requirement that a work is recorded in some permanent form. Three-dimensional works are not protected by copyright, except for artistic works, such as sculpture or architecture, and works of artistic craftsmanship.

Duration

In the case of literary, dramatic, musical and artistic works, protection generally lasts for 70 years after the end of the year in which the author dies. There are exceptions, notably for computer-generated works, which are only protected for 50 years after the end of the year in which they were created.

No registration

Copyright arises automatically on creation, and in the UK and many other jurisdictions there is no need for registration. There are exceptions, most notably in the United States for certain purposes. As an unregistered right, copyright does not protect against independent creation of the same or a similar work, provided that there is no copying involved.

Computer software qualifies for copyright protection as a literary work. This stretches the right somewhat and produces a rather unsatisfactory result. It means that copyright protects the way that code is written, as opposed to the underlying concepts, which are often more valuable. There is a certain amount of overlap between concept and expression, but not much.

Copyright also protects manuals (in whatever form they are produced), the structure, the collection of data and items of data in databases, and the contents of websites.

Moral rights

With certain notable exceptions, authors of copyright works have moral rights. These rights are, broadly, the right to be identified as the author; the right to object to derogatory treatment of a work; the right not to have a work falsely attributed; and the right to privacy of certain films and photographs. Exceptions to these rights include computer programs and computer-generated works. Employees have limited moral rights. Moral rights cannot be transferred but they can be waived.

Database right

Database right protects the collection of data in a database, provided that the data is arranged in a systematic and methodical way and it is individually accessible by electronic or other means. The right lasts for 15 years from the end of the year in which it is completed or the end of the year when it is made available to the public, if that happens before completion.

Databases must be original. The database must be sufficiently original to 'constitute the author's own intellectual creation'. There is a further requirement that there has been a substantial investment in obtaining, verifying or presenting the contents of the database.

Database right is another unregistered right, which arises automatically and can be circumvented by independent creation of a similar database.

Patents

What is patentable?

Patents protect new inventions that make an inventive step beyond the current technology and which are of use to industry. Some types of invention, such as software and business methods, are unpatentable as such, but they can still be patented if there is another facet of the invention that is patentable.

So, for example, word-processing software is viewed as plain software, but software that has a technical effect, such as control software used in a car, may still be patentable. An appreciable amount of software is now patented, and some of the large software providers have a considerable number of patents.

As a registered right a patent can be exceedingly powerful, so there are strict requirements for validity. In industrialized countries, inventions are generally unpatentable if they have been disclosed to anybody, with limited exceptions such as certain confidential disclosures. As regards the inventive step, it must be something that would not be obvious to a highly skilled but unimaginative worker in the field.

Patents and applications contain a description of the invention together with 'claims', which set out the features of the invention that merit registration. They generally last for 20 years from the date when the application was filed, subject to payment of renewal fees. Patents are always subject to revocation on the grounds that they do not meet the requirements for patentability. In the territories where they are granted, they provide a monopoly within the scope of the claims.

Formalities

Applications for patents must be made for each territory where protection is required. There are international filing systems that assist with delivering the applications and it is possible to postpone dealings with national patent offices for around 30 months.

After patents are filed there is usually a search to determine whether the invention is novel. This is followed by examination of the application in each patent office where the application is made, to see whether the invention meets the requirements for patentability. At this stage the scope of the claims may be reduced as a result of negotiation with the examiner.

As a result of this procedure and the requirement for translations patenting can be costly, especially large-scale international filings. However, a patent is the best means of protection for a great many inventions and can be very valuable.

Confidential information

In England, it is possible to protect confidential information, such as secret formulae and sensitive commercial information. Protection arises automatically if the information is genuinely confidential but it is lost if the information ceases to be confidential. It is possible to get an injunction to prevent disclosure but after information has become widely known you can only claim damages for the unauthorized disclosure.

Proving that information is confidential and that disclosure is unauthorized can be difficult, but it is much easier if you have a contract that says that it is confidential and that it must not be disclosed.

Strictly speaking, confidential information is not intellectual property.

Trade marks

What is registrable?

In the UK and the EU, trade marks protect signs that indicate the origin of goods and services. They are not confined to word marks and logos. Provided that they can be represented graphically they can even be smells and jingles. It is also possible to obtain protection for a three-dimensional object, although many applications for shape marks have been refused.

In principle, anything may be registered provided that it is capable of distinguishing the goods of the trade mark owner. However, if a mark is descriptive of the goods themselves it may be refused registration. Registration may also be refused if a mark is too close to a mark that is already registered or if use of the mark could lead to passing off (see below).

Infringement

Trade marks provide a limited monopoly. They can be used to prevent others from using the same mark on the same goods or services, or, if there is a possibility of confusion, a similar mark with similar goods or services. Well-known marks can also be infringed if they are used on different goods that would not be confused where, without due cause, the use would take unfair advantage of the mark or be detrimental to it.

Formalities

As with patents, an application needs to be made in each territory where protection is required and there are international conventions that assist with this. In addition to national marks in the EU, there is a separate Community mark that covers the entire EU. In the UK, trade marks are renewable every 10 years, but may last indefinitely. Like patents they are always subject to revocation on the grounds that they no longer meet the requirements for registration.

Passing off

Passing off is a right that protects goodwill. Technically, there must be a misrepresentation made in the course of trade to existing or prospective customers that is calculated to injure the goodwill of an enterprise and is likely to cause damage.

This is not as complicated as it sounds. It usually involves one business trying to persuade customers of another that they are one and the same so that the clients of the first business will buy from the second. Selling lemon juice in a plastic lemon that was suspiciously similar to another trader's packaging has been sufficient to give rise to a claim for passing off.

Like confidential information, it is not, strictly, an intellectual property right, but it can be very useful for protecting unregistered trade marks and get-up, and there are no formalities. However, lesser-known enterprises may have difficulty in demonstrating sufficient goodwill to take action.

Designs

Currently there are so many rights protecting designs that it can be confusing. There are two types of right under UK law which are valid in the UK only: design rights and registered designs. Under European law, which is applicable throughout the EU including the UK, there is a new registered community design and a community design right.

UK registered designs

Scope

This protection is similar to the registered community design that is described below.

Registered designs protect the appearance of the whole or part of a product resulting from features of lines, contours, colours, shapes, textures and/or materials, and/or ornamentation in particular. It even covers graphic symbols such as computer icons, typographic typefaces, packaging, and get-up.

This right does not protect parts of objects that are hidden from view during normal use, or features of objects that fit mechanically around other objects so that either object may perform its function.

Novelty and individual character

Designs must be 'new' and have 'individual character' in order to qualify for protection. For these purposes 'new' means that it has not been disclosed prior to the previous 12 months in such a way that it would become known to specialists in the industry sector within the community. It is unwise to take advantage of this 12-month period, in case somebody else makes a similar design during that period.

Formalities

Registered design rights may be granted on application to the UK Patent Office. Rights last for a maximum of 25 years provided that they are renewed every 5 years. In common with patents and trade marks, registered designs are subject to revocation on the grounds that they do not fulfil the requirements for registration. As a registered right, the protection provides a monopoly within the registered specification, although the scope of that monopoly may well be interpreted narrowly, more especially in very popular forms of design. Registered design protection is available in many other territories.

UK design right

A design right is an unregistered right that is peculiar to the UK. It protects aspects of shape and configuration (whether internal or external) of the whole or part of an article. It does not protect surface decoration, parts of articles that are designed to fit around other objects, or which are designed to match other objects, or principles of construction.

In the context of computers, a modified form of this right protects semiconductor topographies (i.e. chip designs). It can also protect the shape of new equipment, such as a mouse with an unusual shape.

The right lasts for 15 years from the end of the year in which the design was first recorded in a design document or an article was made to the design, whichever happened first. This 15-year period is reduced if articles made to the design are legitimately marketed in the first 5 years, in which case the right lasts for 10 years from the date of the first sale or hire. Anybody can apply to the Patent Office (officially to the Comptroller of Patents) for a licence during the last five years of the right.

Community designs

There is a registered Community design, which covers the same scope as UK registered designs (see above) but which extends across the entire EU.

Unregistered Community designs, which also apply throughout the EU, are similar to the registered variety, although they only last for three years from the date when they are first made available to the public within the Community. If the design becomes known to specialists in the design sector concerned, then for these purposes, it is deemed to be available to the public.

The unregistered right is intended to protect designs that are short-lived. Like the registered right, designs must be new and have individual character. A design does not qualify for protection unless it is made available to the public. So the first person to disclose a design is entitled to any unregistered design right, although somebody who develops the design independently and not by copying can still use the design.

Taking advice

You will need to take advice from a specialist intellectual property practitioner. If you do not know of one, the Law Society should be able to help you to find one. There are other sources of this information, but they are not always reliable.

7 Source Code Escrow

GRAHAM WOOD

This chapter explains what escrow is and outlines the situations in which you should consider setting up an escrow arrangement.

INTRODUCTION

The word 'escrow' describes an arrangement under which an item is deposited with an agent for delivery to a third party only after the fulfilment of certain conditions.

This type of transaction has been used for hundreds of years to facilitate deals where there is a time lag between the initial stages and completion. Property transfers are a good example of this. The seller wants to know that the purchaser's funds are sufficient and available before completing and handing over the relevant documentation. By placing the funds with a 'trusted third party' who guarantees the amount and that it will be transferred upon receipt of the property transfer documents, this requirement is satisfied.

Whilst escrow is used by the software industry in the manner explained below, there are numerous applications of this process. For example if a company provides services to a business using proprietary financial models developed to assist in its decision-making process, it may well be prudent to request that these models be placed in escrow in the event that the services terminate abruptly.

THE IMPORTANCE OF ESCROW FOR SOFTWARE USERS

Escrow has been used in the IT sector for over 20 years to provide users of software with long term security. The service is built upon the split between source code and object code.

Programmers write software in source code – a form of computer program that is readily understood by humans and is required in order to maintain and update the software. When a program is ready, a compiler converts it into executable or object code – the machine-readable form of the computer program, which is licensed to users. The compiler may be available commercially or the owner may develop it especially for the program.

Software owners normally grant users a licence to use the executable code of their programs. Only very rarely will access to source code be provided as this is normally guarded jealously by the owner. The reason why owners wish to keep their source code secret lies with the legal protection provided for software infringement.

International protection for software is provided by copyright. Copyright provides owners with the right to copy the 'work' and enables them to take action against any infringement. This right depends upon the copy being 'materially' the same as the original. If the source code was to be made public any competitor would be able to see how the code was created and may be able to use this information to quickly (and cheaply) create a similar program. Having to prove in court that this new version is a copy of the original would be expensive and time-consuming. It is therefore far better to keep the source code secret and never to allow this situation to arise.

Source code is necessary in order to maintain and update the software. By ensuring that it remains confidential, the owners prevent users from doing this work themselves. This creates a business risk for the users, as they are then reliant upon the owner for the correct and continuing operation of the software. If the package is key to their business and the owner for some reason is no longer able to support the package, operations may be critically affected.

There are only two realistic options available to the user in this scenario. They can seek access to the source code by paying an additional sum to the owner or they can request a source code escrow agreement.

Source code escrow agreements – also known as source code deposit agreements – provide for the placing of the source code with an independent trusted third party, known as the escrow agent. This agreement, which is made between the owner, the licensee and the escrow agent, states the events under which the source code will be released to the licensee and what the licensee may do with it once he receives it.

WHEN DO YOU NEED ESCROW?

Source code escrow is not necessary for every software package that you purchase. It is likely that relatively few packages used by your organization will meet the requirements for implementing such an arrangement. In any event, looking at software you already use is often too late, as owners are usually reluctant to enter into escrow arrangements after the licence has been signed (see below). It is far easier to request escrow during the negotiations leading to the purchase of a licence.

You should address the following points when considering escrow:

- The software owner:
  - Is the owner a substantial company that is highly unlikely to cease trading or is it a small start-up that could find itself in difficulties very quickly?

Type and scope of software	Type of supplier	Stability of software	Need for escrow
Standard package used across the company	Large multinational software company	Very stable: no maintenance is required and new versions and upgrades appear as a matter of course	Unnecessary: little risk of the owner ceasing to trade; the owner is unlikely to agree to such arrangement.
Standard package; not critical but used daily	Successful specialist software company	Stable: no maintenance is required but upgrades are necessary to address issues	Unnecessary: low risk of the owner ceasing to trade; little business risk if it does. If you do want escrow, it may be worthwhile contacting the user group in order to co-ordinate efforts and minimize costs.
Specialist package; critical to your business	Large specialist software company	Stable: no maintenance is required and you do not use the infrequent upgrades; the owner will not give assurances that the version you use will continue to be maintained	Important: high risk to your business if the owner ceases to trade. Ensure that escrow is addressed prior to entering into a licence agreement so that you have sufficient leverage to require escrow as part of the arrangements.
Specialist package; critical to your business	Small software start-up company	Unstable	Essential: high risk that the owner may go out of business or cease to be able to support and maintain the software.
Bespoke package developed specifically for your company	Software consultancy or contractor	Unstable and untested	Essential: you own the code, so should have copies of it in case you need to continue the development yourself or with a new contractor. Source code escrow offers a solution if you do not wish to manage the receipt and checking of source code from the contractor.

- If it is a smaller company is it backed by a large organization that will step in and pick up the pieces in the event of a problem?
- The software:
  - If you do not accept the latest version of the software from the owner will the one that you have continue to be maintained?
  - Is there an alternative software package on the market that you could quickly switch to with little difficulty?
  - Are there regular maintenance issues with the software?
  - What is the intended life span of the software?
- Your business:
  - Is the software key to your business?
  - Will it cost a large amount to switch software in the event of a problem with the owner?
  - Do you have resource within your organization to use the source code if it was released to you?

TECHNICAL CONSIDERATIONS

Merely being able to access the source code may not be sufficient. Software source code is often immensely complex and completely unintelligible to the layman. Even an expert will usually find it difficult to understand the source code of a complex program if he is not familiar with it. So the question arises as to what you can do with it when it has been released to you?

There will always be packages that your own in-house staff will be able to use, especially if the owner has adhered to accepted quality standards when creating the code and lodged appropriately detailed information. For other situations, it is worthwhile considering the circumstances in which releases are usually made.

Almost all software releases under escrow agreements are made due to the insolvency or cessation of trading of the owner. In these circumstances, the people who wrote the source code will usually be looking for work and it is likely that they would be willing to be contracted to provide support. During this period of support you will be able to ensure that your own staff become familiar with the package so that self-sufficiency is finally attained.

As stated, source code is often immensely complex and even for a relatively straightforward program can run to thousands of pages. For anyone to understand the code (other than its author), it is essential that certain quality controls are used such as proper indentation and notes. Failure to do this can make a huge difference if someone new has to try to work with the package.

VERIFICATION

During the early days of source code escrow, no checks were made on the material deposited with the agents. Eventually it was realized that this was a substantial area of risk as it meant that the effectiveness of the escrow arrangements relied upon the honesty and efficiency of the software owner. From the perspective of the owner, escrow is an added cost that provides little or no benefit. Owners are not usually willing to put much effort into the process, which should be a cause for concern to the user. Verification addresses some of these issues. Verification takes a number of forms. At a basic level, a check is made to ensure that:

- the package contains the number of files expected;
- the code is source code, is correctly indented and has full notes;
- the code is not encrypted or password protected;
- there are no viruses;
- there are no obvious third-party software packages.

You will note that at no stage does this basic level of verification provide any assurance that the code provided is the source code for the package that you are using.

The most effective way to ensure that the code lodged is the required code is to watch the source code being compiled into the executable code. The source should then be handed to the escrow agent whilst the executable is given to the user for testing. If the latter code conforms to the package specification then it is very likely that the source code is the one required by the user. You will receive no guarantees from the escrow agent about this, however, as they do not have access to all the information that would allow them to discern this information.

WHAT SHOULD BE LODGED?

The source code alone is not normally sufficient to be able to support and maintain software. You should also ensure that the following items are considered:

- Full details of the material deposited including the name and version number and the number of items.
- The owner will have used a compiler to compile the source code into executable code. In order to reproduce the executable code, you must identify the exact version of the compiler. If it is not commercially available (it may have been developed specifically for the licensed software by the owner), you will need to have it lodged in escrow as well. If developed by a third party you will need their consent.
- The technical details that will enable someone to access and understand the contents of the media including the file and archive format

and the list or retrieval commands. The type of hardware necessary and the operating system details should also be provided.

- Names and versions of development tools.
- The names and contact details of the people who wrote the original code. If the developer ceases to trade they may then be contacted to provide support on a contract basis.
- Supporting materials such as design notes, flow charts, written documentation, etc. Anything that will assist a trained programmer in understanding the code that is lodged.
- Code developed by third parties and used in the software. Often third-party developers are used to provide specialist elements of packages. If this occurs, then the appropriate source code for this element should also be provided and the consent of its owner obtained to the escrow arrangement.

THE AGREEMENTS

There are many different types of escrow agreement that have been developed over the years in order to deal with different situations. The simplest one is the three party agreement involving the owner, the user and the escrow agent. Agreements have also been developed to deal with multiple licensing situations.

Notwithstanding the many types of agreement, most escrow agreements contain the same elements:

- Statement of ownership or right to enter into the agreement by the owner. This is key to any escrow agreement. Ownership of the copyright in software belongs to the person creating it unless an assignment has been completed. Many software owners do not realize this and it is not unusual for them to bring in outside contractors to complete specialist parts of a package. Unless the rights have been assigned, those contractors could cause problems at a later date if they find out that a third party has access to their source code.
- The release events. These may be anything that the parties agree upon although most standard agreements contain the following:
  - the insolvency of the developer;
  - a material failure by the developer under any maintenance agreement;
  - an assignment of the software to a third party who does not provide the licensee with similar protection to the current escrow agreement within 14 days of such assignment.
- Liability clause. The escrow agent will not provide any assurance that

the code it holds is correct and relates to the particular version that is licensed.

- Confidentiality. Strict obligations of confidentiality should be entered into so that the source code remains a trade secret of the owner. Notwithstanding that the user has access to the source code this does not mean that it can be made available to the whole world. For example it will still be of value to a liquidator in the event of a liquidation and should therefore be rigorously protected.

- Limitations on use. Strict limitations are normally placed upon the user so that the code may be used only for their own maintenance and support. The user should not be able to start licensing the code and making competing packages.

- Rapid arbitration. If there is a dispute about release or some other critical provision a rapid resolution is essential. The user is not going to want to wait months for release at a time when his business may be in jeopardy.

- Title. Unless there are special circumstances, ownership of the source code will not change merely due to a release of the package to the user. A statement confirming that ownership remains with the original owner is found in most escrow agreements.

USER'S DUTIES

An escrow agreement is only as good as the efforts made by the user to ensure its effectiveness. For example the owner may issue new versions on a regular basis. The escrow agent has no knowledge of these new versions unless the user tells it that they have been received. If this is not done then the agent will hold an out of date, and potentially unusable, version of the source code.

The user must also spend some time ensuring that the material placed in escrow is everything that is needed for support and maintenance of the software. It is too late to correct matters if this is left until after a release event.

CHOOSING AN ESCROW AGENT

It is vital to choose an appropriate escrow agent. Many companies have used a bank or a firm of lawyers as their agent. This is not good practice, as these organizations do not usually have the administrative capacity to correctly maintain an escrow deposit over a period of years. Neither do they usually have the skills to provide any level of verification. An agent should have the legal, technical and administrative personnel to back up the services it offers.

There are professional escrow agents that provide a suitable level of service and these should be used wherever possible. The largest escrow agent in the world is DSI Technology Escrow Services. Whilst DSI do not have an office in the UK they do have facilities for holding code all over Europe and provide a professional level of service to UK clients. The oldest UK operator is the NCC Group, in Manchester. The geographical situation of the escrow agent is often unimportant. Code can be delivered world-wide on almost a 24-hour basis. The software industry is truly global. Decisions on agents should be made on the quality of the services provided and, inevitably, cost.

ADVANTAGES OF ESCROW FOR SOFTWARE OWNERS

Owners often attempt to avoid placing their source code in escrow. There are reasons why they should actively consider offering escrow as standard to all customers:

- Confidence. Placing your code in escrow shows a commitment to your customers. It gives customers confidence in their dealings with you and can be a motivation for them to deal with you rather than another supplier. This is particularly true if the owner is dealing in a new market. A number of software companies when attempting to break into a new geographical market have used escrow in their marketing literature to convince companies that there is a low business risk in dealing with them and that they are committed to such customers in a tangible manner.

- Off-site storage of the complete source code. Whilst off-site storage should be a basic business continuity measure for all owners it is surprising how many do not do this. There have been a number of examples of owners requesting their code back from an escrow agent as they have 'lost' their own copy. Furthermore it is common to find that owners do not have a complete copy of the latest source code stored anywhere as different persons in different parts of the company will hold the source code that they are working on. Placing the source code for a package in escrow can be seen as a useful quality measure to ensure that internal standards are complied with.

- Proof of ownership. Software is protected by copyright and one of the main issues concerning proof of ownership is the date the 'work' was created. By placing the code in escrow, the trusted third party can provide evidence of the date that the code was lodged.

CONCLUSION

There have been some notable examples where organizations have obtained release of source code from an escrow agent and been able to support and maintain it after the respective software owners have ceased trading. There have also been a number of companies that have suffered greatly because a key software owner was unable to continue providing its usual service. These examples prove that source code escrow should be part of any business continuity program.

Decisions concerning source code escrow should not be made without a careful consideration of the surrounding circumstances. Making a decision to have no escrow arrangement is probably better than having entered into an escrow agreement where the code lodged is incorrect or there is no means of using it in the event of release. With the former you know you have a business risk, whereas with the latter you falsely think you have a solution.

8 Outsourcing

JEREMY NEWTON

This chapter outlines some of the basic concepts relevant to business process or technology outsourcing. It also considers some of the common jargon and acronyms that are used in the course of outsourcing transactions.

INTRODUCTION

Outsourcing means different things to different people. Expressions like facilities management, business process outsourcing and application service provision are also used to describe a range of commercial arrangements and they are frequently lumped together under the heading outsourcing. In terms of their subject-matter, though, these expressions all mean subtly different things.

A 'pure' outsourcing relationship involves two key elements: a transfer of assets (for example, computer systems or a property portfolio) from the client to the supplier and the provision of services from the supplier to the client (which may be done using the transferred assets or any other resources that the supplier chooses to use, so long as it can deliver the contracted service to the client).

A facilities management (FM) contract is one where the client's own systems are used by the supplier to deliver services to the client, but without any change of ownership. The assets remain under the ownership and at the premises of the client, with the supplier merely granted access to those systems to the extent necessary to provide the managed service.

Business process outsourcing (BPO) involves the transfer to the supplier of an entire business process, such as finance, accounting or payroll. In other words, it is the running of the entire business function which is transferred, not merely the operation of the technology that supports that function.

Application service provision (ASP) involves the delivery of an IT service by a provider who remotely hosts and manages the applications for its clients. Rather than the client buying a software package and then transferring it to the service provider (as part of a traditional outsourcing arrangement), the supplier purchases large volumes of equipment and software licences and allows its clients to use and access those applications remotely, either over the internet or via dedicated lease lines. (It is similar to the concept of 'bureau services', which has been around since the 1950s.)

The list of specific technologies or business processes that can be outsourced is endless. Common IT functions for outsourcing include telecommunications; application development, support and maintenance; desktop support, helpdesk; and training. Looking at it from the broader BPO angle, though, means considering contracts for the outsourcing of human resources functions, finance, payroll processes, and any other business function.

DEFINING THE SERVICES

The starting point for drafting an outsourcing contract is to define the services to be provided to the client. This service description or specification – together with the setting of the service levels to be achieved – lies at the heart of the outsourcing relationship, so it needs to capture all of the services to be provided by the supplier.

It is difficult to generalize usefully about the drafting of service descriptions: there are heavy academic books written on how to go about writing them and the nature and structure of the service description will of course vary substantially from contract to contract. However, there are a number of points of terminology that may be of assistance in understanding how the service description develops:

- Statement of requirements: this document sets out the client's requirements in detail. It is created unilaterally by the client (probably in conjunction with its technical and commercial advisers) and can be included in the tender documentation against which the contractor will propose its 'technical solution'.

- Technical solution: this is the contractor's proposal for the technology that is to be used to deliver the services – as opposed to the essential description of the services themselves.

- Output specification: service descriptions are commonly expressed in terms of an output specification: a statement of the 'outputs' or deliverables that arise out of the service, rather than a description of the 'inputs' of how that service is to be delivered.

OUTPUTS AND INPUTS

By way of illustration of the distinction between outputs and inputs, imagine that you are negotiating a BPO agreement to outsource your company's accounts department. The services you are looking for may include, say, credit checking and debt collection. As the user, you want to know that credit checks and debt collection are carried out to certain standards.

However, as long as the supplier meets those standards and provides the information required in the agreed form and within agreed timescales, the outsourcing purist will say it is of no interest to you (as the user) whether the supplier performs those functions using the latest high-end servers and the fastest available networks, or whether it does so by scribbling calculations on the back of an envelope.

As long as you are getting the outputs you need, when you need them, and in the correct format, who cares how the supplier gets them to you?

DESIGN RISK

There is often a degree of overlap between outputs and inputs. The client will probably specify the management reports it wants, but also how it wants to receive them – for example, using the interfaces between its own internal systems and the technology used by the supplier to provide the service. However, there is a sound legal reason for the client to separate outputs and inputs: if the client goes into too much detail about the technology, it may thereby approve the technical solution that the contractor has come up with – in other words, it takes back the 'design risk' that the supplier would normally bear. If the technical infrastructure fails completely, the supplier will argue that the client had approved the solution and accordingly has to live with the consequences of its non-performance.

It may be that certain inputs in the technical solution are important enough to form a mandatory part of the service description, but these are normally limited to those parts of a solution which the client considers to be so crucial to the delivery of the services that they have to be stated expressly.

Of course, the intention of transferring the design risk will vary from contract to contract. That is certainly the orthodox approach in relation to many public sector and PFI contracts, but it may be different in relation to outsourcing agreements involving, say, defence companies or banks. In these cases, there are very sophisticated IT departments who want to retain a significant degree of control over the way the contractor delivers the services to the business.

SERVICE LEVEL AGREEMENT

Once the parties have defined what the services are, they can then move on to the next big commercial issue: how well are the services to be performed?

This is defined in a Service Level Agreement (SLA). The SLA part of an outsourcing agreement has four main aspects:

- it defines the service levels to be achieved;
- it sets out targets for those service levels;
- it prescribes the mechanism for monitoring and reporting actual service levels against those targets;
- it addresses the consequences of failure to meet those targets (which may include, for example, payment of rebates or service credits).

SLAs are discussed in more detail in Chapter 1. However, the following terminology crops up frequently in the specific context of outsourcing:

- Performance points: An SLA usually combines a variety of service levels and many agreements have literally dozens of performance indicators, all of which may have implications in terms of financial compensation or termination. One of the ways of handling the (potentially very complicated) arithmetic is to set up a system of 'performance points': instead of stating that the remedy for a particular breach consists of a service credit of X percent of the charges, you say that the defect attracts Y performance points. Other service levels similarly attract performance points, and of course the number of points attributable to a particular deficiency can be weighted so as to emphasize the more important service levels and reduce the impact of the minor ones. At the end of the relevant measurement period, the total number of performance points is calculated and the service credit is based on the number of performance points (so N performance points amounts to a rebate of X percent of the periodic charge). A further refinement would be that if the number of performance points in a given period exceeds a given figure, then the matter is escalated between the parties and may give rise to termination.

- Performance indicators and key performance indicators: The number of service levels to be achieved will vary from contract to contract. It is important that complexity is not built into the SLA for its own sake: just because a particular metric can be measured does not mean that it need be measured. In some contracts, the parties undertake to comply with unbelievably complicated performance regimes which are likely to be totally unworkable in practice because of the number and frequency of reports, the complexity of the arithmetic, and so on. For this reason, a distinction is often drawn between performance indicators (PIs) and key performance indicators (KPIs) to clarify which measures of service need to be reported on just as a matter of interest or good management practice, and which give rise to contractual exposure in the event of failure.

- Ratchet mechanisms: A simple ratchet mechanism increases the number of performance points awarded for a particular failure if the defect occurs too often within a specified period. For example, if X points are awarded for a failure to achieve a particular output, then if that failure recurs more than three times in the relevant period, each subsequent occasion attracts 2X points. The aim is to encourage the contractor to rectify service defects by increasing the stakes for successive occurrences of a defect. A ratchet mechanism may be used in connection with a non-key performance indicator, where the level of financial impact from failure to perform is not sufficient to encourage the contractor to improve but is potentially inconvenient for clients or users.

ELEMENTS OF AN SLA

The performance regime needs to be built from the ground up. Start by defining what you are trying to measure and work from there to set the targets, the means of measuring performance and the consequences of failure. In a contract for the provision of call centre services, for example, the parties may agree that a relevant service level is 'time to connect to an operator'. With that service level agreed, the parties then need to go on to define:

- the target for that service level – for example, 8 seconds for peak and 4 seconds for off-peak calls;
- the mechanism for measuring and reporting – for example, random sampling or continuous monitoring of all calls, averaged out over a 4 week period;
- the consequences of failure – for example, some form of service credits (perhaps on a sliding scale, with credits increasing according to the severity of the deterioration in service) or termination of the agreement.

There needs to be a clear 'read-through' from one part of the SLA to the next, with the various obligations expressed in common terminology and according to an agreed structure. Too often, disputes arise out of ambiguities in the wording of an SLA which in turn derive from the fact that different members of the team have taken responsibility for the various elements, without anyone taking overall control of the SLA.

PRICING AND PAYMENT MECHANISMS

Pricing and payment mechanisms are the commercial heart of the outsourcing contract, but there is little that can be said by way of useful generalizations about these aspects. Basic charging structures may consist of:

- a fixed price for the service per quarter or per year;
- a fixed price per unit of utilized resource (such as £1 per 100 transactions processed);
- 'cost plus' charges, where the supplier is entitled to recover its costs of providing the services, plus an agreed percentage profit margin.

Whatever the general charging arrangements, though, a greater proportion of the time in negotiations is usually spent in devising the mechanism for price variations. Any IT contract should include a change control mechanism (see Chapter 2) as a matter of course. In the context of a 10 year outsourcing agreement – where the technology itself is likely to change dramatically over the lifetime of the contract, even if the client's business does not – how do you build a mechanism that allows the parties sufficient flexibility to improve the delivery of the services without having to stop and re-negotiate the pricing at every turn?

Project open book accounting

Project open book accounting (POBA) principles can be applied to ensure that there is transparency in relation to the accounts and costings for a project. It tends to lead to a better understanding between the parties about the level of costs incurred in delivering the services and so tends to reduce the scope for surprises or debate when changes are being priced under the change control mechanism. POBA can also assist in fostering better, more open, working relationships, which tend to be necessary in the context of the 'partnering' or 'partnership' type of outsourcing agreement.

Naturally, there is some resistance on the part of suppliers about opening their books to the client's scrutiny. It is important to ensure that the use of this information is limited strictly to the scope of the project and also, to avoid the obligations on the contactor becoming too onerous, to limit the client's right of access to its books to once or twice per year. However, giving access to this information will allow the client to undertake its own assessment in relation to estimating the cost of changes and will also provide it with some security against unreasonable estimates for changes.

Benchmarking

Benchmarking is a process by which the contractor compares its charges against the prices for which the client could obtain the same services elsewhere in the market. If the relevant costs are higher than market costs, then the contractor makes a reduction in the price charged to the client, subject to some agreed cost-sharing ratio. If costs are lower than market costs, the contractor may seek to come back to the client and try to raise its prices.

Market testing

This is a process that applies particularly to any part of the services that are sub-contracted by the contractor to a third party. The aim is that the contractor re-tenders on the market for the service, in order to test that everybody is getting value for money from that service. If a new sub-contractor does the same work at a lower price, this reduction may be passed on to the client.

Problems with benchmarking and market testing

Benchmarking and market testing are common mechanisms, particularly in large-scale public contracts, but they are unpopular with contractors because one of the reasons for outsourcing is to take advantage of the economies of scale that the third party offers. Those economies of scale will often be factored into the initial price and the contractor will argue that as long as the client is happy with the initial price, why should it be concerned whether the supplier's profit is greater, or less, or indeed whether it makes no profit at all?[1]

The mechanisms can also be very complex, so unless value for money is of overwhelming importance to you, it may be better to steer clear of them. These mechanisms tend to work better in the context of projects like construction or roads rather than the more subtle (and faster moving) world of IT, where costs tend to drop from year to year.

THE OUTSOURCING LIFE CYCLE

The outsourcing relationship can be a long-term arrangement, involving a number of phases, each of which gives rise to slightly different issues and all of which need to be provided for in the contract paperwork:

- the initial transfer of assets from the client to the service provider;
- the transition of services (and perhaps staff) from the client's organization to the service provider;
- the service delivery phase and continuing service management;
- exit arrangements and/or transition to another service provider.

Initial asset transfer

In terms of the contractual paperwork (as opposed to the commercial discussions), the starting point is the initial transfer of assets. Asset transfer agreements are very commonplace: any commercial lawyer can draft one. Typically, the agreement identifies the assets to be transferred, includes some warranties as to their ownership and condition, and sets out the mechanism for paying the price. However, there is an extra dimension to the asset transfer in the context of outsourcing, because the transaction is not just a one-off.

In the normal contract for the sale of an asset, the main aim of the seller is usually to get the highest price (with the lowest ongoing exposure in terms of guarantees about the condition of the asset). A good example is the sale of a car: the seller is not concerned with the use the buyer makes of the

---

[1] Of course, if the contractor can not make a profit, it will lose interest in performing the services properly. Regardless of the contractual rights and wrongs, this can seriously impact the client's business, for example if all the best contractor staff are moved onto a new and more profitable job.

asset and if the buyer does not make proper use of it, there is normally no adverse impact on the seller.

In the case of outsourcing, however, the buyer is buying the assets for the specific purpose of providing services to the seller, so the price allocated to any asset will be reflected in the charges payable by the client for the services. So the asset transfer has to be seen in the context of the overall outsourcing deal.

The core of the asset transfer is the asset register, the list or schedule of assets that are to move across to the service provider. In the context of technology outsourcing, these will typically include :

- Hardware – which can be identified by reference to manufacturers' names, serial numbers and locations;

- Software licences – which can similarly be identified by reference to the package names and version numbers, and the contract numbers of the licences under which the software is used;

- Other contracts related to the use and support of those assets – for example, support and maintenance agreements, equipment leases, disaster recovery contracts, and employment contracts for the individuals involved with the assets to be transferred. (Most IT operations are underpinned by a web of such contracts and the service provider will want to be assured that it has the benefit of all these contracts on a continuing basis, at least until it has completed a transition of the services from the existing infrastructure to its own.)

As part of gathering this information and ensuring it is complete and correct, the parties will often undertake what is known as a due diligence exercise: this involves identifying all the relevant assets, tracking down any relevant contract paperwork, reviewing all this information (from technical, commercial and legal points of view) and then addressing any problems that come to light. For example, a common problem area is in relation to the assignment of software licences: the standard terms of most large software houses provide that the licensee may only assign the licence if the consent of the software house has been obtained. Even if the software house does not object to the proposed transfer, getting that consent in writing can be very time-consuming, so it is essential that the parties embark on this due diligence exercise at the earliest opportunity, to build up as complete a picture as possible of the assets to be transferred and the risks associated with them.

Transition of services

During the transition phase, the responsibility for the provision of the services moves across from the client (who is effectively 'self-providing' as at the contract date) to the service provider. On the day that the contract is signed, it is unlikely that the service provider will immediately be able to meet the contractual target service levels, so there is often a period – which may be up to a year in contracts requiring major business process re-engineering – during which the service level agreement does not 'bite' to its fullest extent.

During that period, the client and the supplier will need to collaborate to ensure that the supplier has built up a full understanding of the client's business requirements. It may be that the client has to change its business processes to bring them into line with the recommendations by the supplier in order to achieve promised business benefits. The contract should include a detailed transition plan which states clearly each party's rights and obligations with regard to getting the systems and the services up and running, the timetable for achieving full service delivery, and so on.

Service delivery phase

At the end of the transition phase, the supplier should be in a position to deliver the services to meet the contracted service levels. The contract then moves into a new phase, which concerns ongoing service management. Typically, the outsourcing contract will include a governance model, which describes how the relationship between the parties is to be managed during the service delivery period and includes periodic service reviews to consider both historic performance and any service improvements that may be required. Note that these review arrangements need to be dovetailed closely with the change control procedures.

Exit arrangements

The final stage of the outsourcing life cycle is termination. Whether the contract expires because it reaches the end of its agreed term or is terminated before that point, the client must ensure that there is an agreed and contractually binding exit plan. This will typically require the service provider to assist the client in getting the services (and any relevant assets) transferred either to a new service provider or back to the client. The exit plan should be reviewed periodically throughout the service delivery phase to ensure:

- that the supplier maintains an up-to-date register of all the assets it uses to provide the services;
- that all relevant documentation is kept in an orderly fashion, so that the supplier can easily verify matters like ownership of equipment and the transferability of software licences in the event of termination of the outsourcing agreement;
- that any assets that are not freely transferable to the client can at least be used by the client (or a new contractor) for a sufficient period to enable them to move the services over to new assets.

OTHER RELEVANT ISSUES

This chapter has outlined the general shape of a typical outsourcing contract and explained some of the terminology that is often heard in the course of the commercial negotiation. However, there are a couple of important legal areas that it is possible only to touch on in this book.

One issue is the sensitive matter of staff transfers and the Transfer of Undertaking (Protection of Employment) Regulations (TUPE). This law is intended to protect staff when the 'undertaking' they work for is transferred to another organization, as will commonly be the case in outsourcing contracts. Where TUPE applies, the current employment contracts of the staff in that 'undertaking' (which is not necessarily a company or a self-contained business unit) are automatically transferred across to the new organization. In the context of outsourcing, for example, the service provider may become responsible for honouring the contracts of certain client employees, whether it needs them or not. It is essential that TUPE matters are considered as part of the outsourcing discussions and contractual arrangements, but it is not proposed to say more about it here, except that it is essential to obtain specialist legal advice.

Secondly, there is considerable interest at present in offshore outsourcing – for example, moving call centres or back-office functions to India or Eastern Europe. There are often sound economic reasons for making this move, but doing business in a different jurisdiction and time zone is a major step. Common problem areas in international outsourcing include the need to adopt complex corporate or tax structures; difficulties with international dispute resolution and the enforcement of judgments; and unfamiliar laws about ownership and licensing of intellectual property rights. It is essential to obtain specialist legal advice from an adviser with expertise in the relevant field (and jurisdiction) before taking such a significant step.

9 Data Protection

ANDREW KATZ

Data protection is a complex area. It is notoriously difficult to summarize, because the legislation is so full of exemptions, provisos and exceptions. This chapter aims to give the reader a working knowledge of the overall scheme of the legislation and highlight the areas where there are potential pitfalls, so that specialized advice can be sought.

INTRODUCTION

The current law is contained in the Data Protection Act 1998, which is more wide-ranging than the preceding legislation and is still not fully enforced, being phased in over a period of eight years (the Act will be fully in force on 24 October 2007). The legislation is supported by a host of regulations, many of which deal with its piecemeal phasing into force, none of which help the clarity of the position. Luckily, most of these transitions are now over.

The website of the Information Commissioner is always a useful jumping-off point to get to grips with changes in this area. Although the information it gives may occasionally be misleading, it is a good primary source of information, not least because the Information Commissioner is primarily responsible for enforcement of the legislation and should be receptive to the argument that a data controller was following the advice which was published on the official website.

TERMINOLOGY

The words 'data' and 'information' have venerable well-established meanings to those who study information theory and computing. Unfortunately, when Parliament drafted the legislation, it chose to ignore these and almost perfectly interchange the established definitions of 'data' and 'information'. If you have any grounding in information theory, try to ignore what you have been taught when reading this chapter!

In addition, there have been bizarre terminological changes between the first Data Protection Act (1984) and the latest (1998). The post of the Information Commissioner (the current title) was formerly known as the Commissioner for Data Protection, and before that the Data Protection Registrar. Under the 1984 Act, you would 'register' with the 'Registrar' which would result in you holding a 'registration'. However, you now 'notify' with the 'Commissioner' which still leaves you having an entry in the 'register'. The information which you must provide during the notification process is called the 'register of particulars'. There is no compelling reason why the legislation could not have been consistent and just referred to 'registration', 'register', 'registrar' and 'registrable particulars'.

WHAT DATA ARE COVERED

In a nutshell, the Data Protection Act ensures that any personal data (i.e. any data relating to a living individual) are only obtained, processed and held by entities (called 'data controllers') which have notified (i.e. 'registered') with the Information Commissioner. 'Data subjects' have a right to know who holds data about them, what that data are, that the data are used properly and for specified purposes, and they are not used in a way that can harm them. In addition, the data controller is obliged to take steps to ensure that the information is secure, and is not disclosed to unauthorized persons. Data subjects have various rights, including the right to compensation should a data controller fail to comply with obligations under the Act.

It is vital to understand what is meant by 'personal data'. The definition in the Act says that personal data means data which relate to a living individual who can be identified from those data, or from those data and other information which is in the possession of or is likely to come into the possession of the data controller. Names are personal data. Names and addresses together are personal data (although the addresses themselves are probably not). Email addresses in the form andrew.katz@moorcrofts.com are personal data, but 12345.1234@compuserve.com are not. Information about George V is not personal data because he is dead. Information about companies (as long as it does not refer to members of staff, directors or other individuals) is not personal data because companies are not individuals.

There are some serious problems, however, with these definitions. For example, the proviso about data being personal data if it identifies a living individual in conjunction with other information which is in the possession of or is likely to come into the possession of the data controller. Every office has a set of telephone directories. A telephone directory is a catalogue of names, addresses and telephone numbers: clearly personal data. If someone in the office holds an address or a telephone number in isolation, it may be a phenomenally difficult task to go through the telephone directory searching for the telephone number or the address to see whose name tallies up with it, but it is possible. In general, therefore, all email addresses, street addresses and telephone numbers should be regarded as personal information, even if their connection with a living individual cannot immediately be identified. Although the Information Commissioner has historically taken the strict view set out in this paragraph, in a recent case (*Durant v. Financial Services Authority* [2003] EWCA Civ 1746) the Court of Appeal determined that this approach was too restrictive and that data are only to be regarded as personal if the focus of the document in question is the data subject (in other words, the data subject is not just named incidentally in the text) so long as the right to privacy of the data subject is maintained and respected. The Commissioner has acknowledged that he must rewrite the guidance on his website during the early part of 2004, and also change the advice and enforcement processes he institutes internally (Information Commissioner 2003).

Images (photographs and videos) of people are capable of qualifying as personal data, if they identify the individual in conjunction with other information held by the data controller or likely to come into its possession. A major effect of this is that closed circuit television systems (CCTV) are essentially data gathering and storage devices and that organizations employing them therefore have to comply with the provisions of the Data Protection Act. This topic is in itself a complex one and further guidance is available on the Commissioner's website.

Do not fall into the trap of assuming that if you do not keep the information on a computer (or if you do not have a database), the Act does not apply to you. Manual data are now covered by the Data Protection Act and with few exceptions any data held in a 'relevant filing system' are covered by the Act. In a nutshell, if a filing system is any use (i.e. if you can actually find the information you are looking for in any meaningful way) then it is a 'relevant filing system'. A filing cabinet containing personnel files ordered alphabetically is a relevant filing system as is an alphabetical address book, for example. Until recently, the Commissioner took the view that manual records accessible in this way are to be treated identically to computer-based records. It now seems likely that the Commissioner's view will become more pragmatic given the case referred to above.

SENSITIVE PERSONAL DATA

One category of personal data, sensitive personal data, is treated more stringently by the Act. Sensitive personal data consist of information which relates to:

- the racial or ethnic origin of the data subject;
- their political opinions;
- their religious beliefs or other beliefs of a similar nature;
- whether they are a member of a trade union;
- their physical or mental health or condition;
- their sexual life;
- the commission or eventual commission by them of any offence;
- any proceedings for any offence committed or alleged to have been committed by them, the disposal of such proceedings or the sentence of any court in such proceedings.

In general, the data controller has to take particular care when dealing with sensitive personal data. There are some obligations under the Act which are more stringent when relating to sensitive personal data, than when they relate to other (non-sensitive) personal data.

WHO NEEDS TO NOTIFY?

Unless subject to a specific exemption, it is an offence to process personal data without an appropriate entry in the register (called 'notification'). The exemptions include individuals who process personal data for personal, family or household affairs (which also exempts domestic data controllers from most of the other provisions of the Act) and, in the context of business:

- staff administration;
- advertising, marketing and public relations;
- accounts and records.

There are also various exemptions from notification for certain non-profit making organizations, including clubs.

There are two important points:

- exemption from notification does not (by itself) mean exemption from the other provisions of the Act;
- the exemptions are fairly narrow and it is often difficult to interpret the exemptions and see whether they specifically apply.

Experience shows that, when most businesses are examined in any detail, they are almost invariably undertaking activities which are outside the scope of the exemptions and are therefore required to notify.

There are, in any event, some advantages to notifying voluntarily, even though it will cost you £35 each year and take a little bit of administration time. It removes the obligation on the data controller (Section 24 of the Act) to supply, free of charge, to anyone requesting it basically the same information that they would have to supply in the notification. It therefore makes more sense to compile this information once for notification purposes, rather than having to do it each time somebody makes a request.

Typical examples as to why the exemptions do not go far enough are:

- Many employers now offer their employees a pension (indeed, with the introduction of stakeholder pensions, this is in many cases compulsory). The administration of these pensions will necessarily involve holding personal data and passing it on to pension trustees, something which is not dealt with in the employee administration exemption.

- Employee records will frequently contain information about an employee's next of kin. Our view is that next of kin data relates to a living individual other than the employee him or herself, and is therefore covered by the exemption (there is some guidance from the Information Commissioner which contradicts this, but in the end it is for the courts, not the Information Commissioner, to determine this).

HOW TO NOTIFY

You can notify on the Information Commissioner's website, by email, by post, or by telephone. The information which is required to undertake a notification is:

- the data controller's name and address;
- the name and address of any representative of the data controller;
- a description of the personal data being or to be processed and the category of data subjects to which they relate;
- a description of the purpose of processing;
- a description of any intended recipients of the data;
- a list of the countries outside the European Economic Area (EEA) that will or may be in receipt of the data from the data controller;
- a statement (if relevant) of the fact that certain data processed by the data controller are of a type excluded from notification.

You must notify under the correct name of the data controller (e.g. if you are a limited company, the proper company name including 'Limited') as well as any names you trade under. If you are a partnership, you should notify under the partnership's trading names as opposed to the names of the individual partners. If you have more than one company in your group processing data (in practice, this is likely to be all non-dormant companies) then they each have to notify separately. Remember that they may be undertaking different processing, so the notifications may need to be different and ensure that there is an entry in the notification allowing for the transfer of personal data between companies in the group.

The notification form also requires you to summarize the steps you have taken to ensure data security. If you have taken measures to guard against unauthorized or unlawful processing of personal data and against accidental loss, destruction or damage, do the methods include:

- adopting an information security policy (i.e. providing clear management direction on responsibilities and procedures in order to safeguard personal data)?
- taking steps to control physical security (e.g. locking doors of the office or building where computer equipment is held)?
- putting in place controls on access to information (e.g. introducing password protection and encryption on files containing personal data)?
- establishing a business continuity plan (e.g. holding a backup file in the event of personal data being lost through flood, fire or other catastrophe)?
- training your staff on security systems and procedures?
- detecting and investigating breaches of security when they occur?

- adopting the British Standard on Information Security Management BS7799? (This standard is not a statutory requirement but a business-led approach to best practice on information security management.)

See the section on Data Protection Principle 7 later in this chapter for more information about the security of personal data.

The Commissioner has made it much easier to notify by drawing up a set of templates for a number of different types of business which contain the elements of notification most likely to apply to that business. These are available on the Commissioner's website and are by far the easiest way to commence a notification. Be careful, however, because they are not comprehensive and it is unlikely that any specific business fits precisely within a template. They are very useful as a guide but do not use them without thinking through the issues and, especially, about whether there are other areas not contained within the template which need to be covered.

For example, none of the templates contains a notification relating to the issue of personal data to potential investors or successor businesses of a data controller. In practice, many businesses are in the market for acquisition or wish to raise finance; as part of that process they will have to undergo due diligence. This due diligence will almost certainly result in personal data being made available to a potential successor business or investor but, in the absence of a specific notification permitting that disclosure, it would be a criminal offence to release the information to them. The Information Commissioner's office has suggested that data provided in due diligence can be made anonymous but, in the context of most small- to medium-sized businesses, this would not be feasible. It is important, therefore, to think through the processes involved in your business and potential business developments to determine the scope of an appropriate notification.

Many businesses make the mistake of thinking that once they have notified, they can go ahead and process data in whatever way they like. Notification is just the first step. Businesses still have to comply with the data protection principles in relation to the data that they hold, process and disclose, and, in particular, this may mean that they may need to obtain the consent of the data subjects before undertaking that processing.

You are required to renew your notification annually and if the nature of the business changes so that there would be any changes to your notification, you are under an obligation to notify the Information Commissioner of those changes.

THE PRINCIPLES OF DATA PROTECTION

Personal data must be:
1. fairly and lawfully processed;
2. processed for limited purposes;
3. adequate, relevant and not excessive;
4. accurate;
5. not kept longer than necessary;
6. processed in accordance with the data subject's rights;
7. secure;
8. not transferred to countries without adequate protection.

The full text of the principles is set out in Schedule 1 to the Act, together with some additional interpretation.

DATA PROTECTION PRINCIPLES

1. Fair and lawful processing

'Processing' includes almost any activity involving data: obtaining them, retrieving them, analysing them, performing actions on them and disclosing them. That means that for the processing to be lawful, the data must have been obtained fairly and lawfully in the first place. Where you are obtaining the data from the data subject him or herself, you must ensure that the data are obtained fairly (i.e. you disclose who you are, why you need the data, and what you are going to do with them). If you are obtaining it from a third party, things are more complicated.

When you obtain data from a person other than the data subject, there are essentially two scenarios. Either you have obtained the information from a person providing information about someone else (e.g. an airline obtains personal data about a passenger from the travel agent booking the ticket) or you have obtained the information from a third-party database (e.g. a mailing list broker).

In each case, you must (so far as is practicable) as soon as possible after obtaining the data, provide the data subject in question with certain details (i.e. who you are, why you have the data, and what you are going to do with them). 'So far as is practicable' are the words used in the legislation and there is as yet no guidance from the courts as to how that will be interpreted.

In practical terms, this means that if you are harvesting data from individuals, you should always ask them whether they are the data subject in question (for example, if your call centre takes calls from customers over the phone and a caller gives a credit card in the name of Annabel Smith, you should ask the caller if they are Annabel Smith, and challenge them if they appear to have a male voice or sound too young to have a credit card – but this is good security practice anyway). If the person providing the data turns out not to be the data subject, you should ensure that you provide the actual data subject with the necessary information.

If you get the data from a mailing list, you will need to satisfy yourself that the list broker obtained the data fairly and lawfully; that it can lawfully pass the data on to you and that you can lawfully use the data you obtain for the purposes you want to use them for. If the list broker did not obtain the data fairly and lawfully, you cannot make use of them without breaching the Act, so you need to be absolutely sure that you can use the list and build strong protection (e.g. indemnity clauses) protecting you against any claims that the list cannot be used lawfully.

You should ask the list broker some difficult questions about how they obtained the data:

- Did you obtain the data yourself or from a third party?
- Do you know that the data subjects themselves provided you with the data and not someone on their behalf?
- Do you have the consent of the data subjects to release their details to me? How was that consent obtained?
- Do you have the consent of the data subjects to use their names for the purposes I am contemplating?
- How do you handle updates and corrections to the list? Can I have access to your updates and corrections for the period of the list hire?
- How do you handle requests from the data subjects for their names not to be used for marketing purposes?

Any reputable list-broking firm should be able to provide answers to these questions to your satisfaction.

2. Processing for limited purposes

Data should be processed only for the purposes which you have notified the Information Commissioner and, where you need consent for processing, only for the purposes for which you have consent. For example, if you have obtained data from customers for billing purposes, you must not, in the absence of consent from those customers, use the data for marketing to them. It is therefore important to convey to data subjects, when you are harvesting data, the purposes for which you want the data and to obtain their consent to the use of the data for those purposes.

WHEN IS CONSENT NOT CONSENT?

One of the characteristics which makes processing 'fair' is that you have the data subject's consent to the processing. Where the data involved are 'sensitive personal data' then the Act says that 'explicit consent' is required. This means that the data subject must agree, in some unequivocal way, to the processing taking place and, logically, that they are fully informed as to what they are consenting to.

In other words, the data subject must be made aware of the purposes for which their data are to be processed; and must indicate that they give their consent. The consent can be in writing, or spoken, or even a tick in a box. However, giving the data subject the right to opt out (as opposed to opting in) in these circumstances is not sufficient. For example, a box saying 'tick here if you do NOT want your sensitive personal data processed for marketing purposes' would not be sufficient to ensure that the processing was fair.

Lawyers, therefore, assume that for other personal data the consent required does not need to be explicit, and therefore can be implicit. What is implied consent? If someone leaves their name and address details after telephoning a 'catalogue order line' voicemail, then clearly they have implied consent to use their address details to send them a catalogue. It is questionable whether they have implied consent to anything else done with those data, however.

It is arguable, but it is probably implied consent if a data subject fails to tick the box on a reply form which says 'tick here if you do NOT want us to make your details available to other companies for marketing purposes'. In other words, for non-sensitive data, opt-outs are (probably) permissible.

The question of whether implied consent has been given will depend in each case on the circumstances given.

3. Adequate, relevant and not excessive

This principle is self-explanatory. You must obtain the appropriate data you need to carry out your job properly (for example, as a credit reference agency you would need to ensure that you have adequate data about a data subject to be able to make a decision as to their creditworthiness). You must only collect relevant data (it is not necessary, for example, to collect data on the inside leg measurement of your customer if you are in the business of pizza delivery). However, it is very easy for you (or your web designers) to ask irrelevant questions when harvesting data from websites, for example. Think whether it is necessary for you to know the age, sex or marital status of your customers? In many cases, the answer will be 'yes' but at least give the data subjects a chance to opt out of providing that information. In practice, so long as the data you hold is relevant, then it is difficult to see how it would be 'excessive'.

4. Accurate

Keeping your data accurate makes good business sense. The amount of effort you invest in keeping your data accurate should be balanced against both the importance to you of keeping your data accurate and the potential harm which the data subject could suffer. For example, if you hold medical records, an incorrect reference that the data subject is not allergic to penicillin could clearly be disastrous. Likewise, if you are a credit reference agency holding incorrect data showing a data subject to be an undischarged bankrupt, you are liable for damages to the data subject for any loss or distress caused by a bad credit rating. If however, you are the proprietor of a pop singer's web site you may be able to argue that the data subject's favourite colour needs somewhat less care. In practical terms, the data most companies will think about in the context of data protection are marketing and contact data and employment records; in both cases, it is sensible to have a regular review of the data you hold to ensure that it is kept up-to-date and accurate. The Commissioner is likely to be less sympathetic to data subjects' claims that your data was inaccurate if you make it easy for data subjects to correct any errors: for example, providing a page on the website for reviewing and amending details, or sending out an update form with the data subject's details and inviting them to amend any errors. In the latter case, do not be tempted (as several financial institutions have done recently) to send out a letter along the lines of 'We know you have opted out of marketing so we are writing to ensure that we are holding accurate details about you and to remind you of what wonderful services we can offer you'.

THE RIGHT TO OPT OUT OF MARKETING

The Act ensures that data subjects can opt out of the use of their details for direct marketing purposes. In practical terms, you should ensure that you have a mechanism available to log any objections by data subjects to the use of their data for direct marketing purposes and either delete their names from your database or, if you need to keep the data for other purposes, make sure you have a flag on the database which marks those records which must not be used for direct marketing. There is also an argument that you should maintain a database of people who have objected to direct marketing, so that you can cross-check it against any data you obtain subsequently, to ensure that you do not start processing a data subject's details for direct marketing after they have sent you a notice requiring you to stop (and you have removed their name from the main database).

There are a number of stop lists (such as the Mailing Preference Service) to which data subjects may submit their names. Companies may obtain copies of these lists by signing up with the appropriate bodies and use them to purge their databases of the details of people who do not want the data used for direct marketing purposes. The Mailing Preference Service is a voluntary (i.e. non-statutory and non-compulsory) scheme but good business sense suggests using such a service (on the basis that sending direct mail to someone who has subscribed to the list will be a waste of a stamp and may lead to a vocal opponent of your company). The service has been available since 1983, well before the advent of any data protection legislation in the UK.

The Direct Marketing Association, which runs the Mailing Preference Service and the Email Preference Service, was also appointed by Oftel (now Ofcom) to administer the Fax Preference Service and the Telephone Preference Service, which were implemented in 1999. These two schemes are statutory and operate under the Telecommunications (Data Protection and Privacy) Regulations 1999 (Statutory Instrument 1999 No. 2093). Prior to undertaking any fax shots or unsolicited telephone marketing, you must remove from your target list any names which appear on the appropriate stop lists maintained by the DMA or be at risk of committing a criminal offence. Copies of the lists are obtainable from the DMA (a fee is payable). Note that it is illegal to contact private individuals by fax for direct marketing purposes without their consent, irrespective of whether they are on the stop list.

The Privacy and Electronic Communications (EC Directive) Regulations 2003 limit the use of unsolicited text messages or emails. In a nutshell, if you propose to send commercial text or email messages to an individual subscriber (including a partnership), you need to ensure either that you have a pre-existing business relationship with them (i.e. you are responding to an enquiry or you have supplied them with similar goods or services to the ones about which you are emailing) or that they have expressly consented (i.e. opted in) to receiving marketing information from you. Unsolicited commercial emails should always be clearly identified as such and should allow the recipient an easy way to opt out of receiving them.

It is also worth bearing in mind the Code of Advertising Practice (CAP) which makes it a necessity for corporate bodies, as well as individuals, to opt-in to receiving unsolicited commercial emails. Although not legally binding, failure to comply with the CAP can lead to a business being blacklisted and therefore unable to advertise in participating media. Taking this into account together with the difficulty in determining whether a 'subscriber' is an individual, a partnership or a company, many commentators are saying that the best advice is only to send unsolicited commercial emails where there is a positive opt-in, irrespective of whether the recipient is a company, a partnership or an individual.

The 2003 regulations also regulate the use of cookies. A cookie is a small piece of data which is stored on a user's computer at the request of the web server hosting a website which the user is viewing. They are designed to have a benign purpose – to enable the web server to retrieve the state of the website when the user last visited, for example. They are often used to store shopping carts, details about favourite items and to enable a web server to identify who a particular user is without them having to log in. Used in this way, they improve the user experience significantly. However, they can also be used to track a user's movements around the site and to gather various other pieces of information. The 2003 regulations require a web site to alert the user to the use of cookies and to allow the user to disable them.

5. Not kept longer than necessary

This heading is, at first sight, self-explanatory but it raises some difficulties. Your auditors will no doubt insist that you keep financial data for at least seven years (and it is an obligation under the self-assessment tax regime to do so). However, this is likely to include personal data. The Information Commissioner may argue that you should make the data anonymous, to the extent that you can without breaching the requirements of your auditors and the Inland Revenue, but in practice that is likely to be impossible. You may also want to keep other data for at least six years in case of legal action (the 'statute of limitations' generally allows you to sue and be sued up to six years from the event complained of) – indeed your insurers may place an obligation like this on you. This highlights the need to ensure that your notification covers all the purposes for which you may need to retain data and to maintain a constant review of the data you hold to ensure that you delete any data which are no longer required.

This poses a special problem so far as backups are concerned: many companies will have a dusty cupboard containing backup tapes, possibly in an old format which the company no longer has the equipment available to read. These may contain data which are covered by the Act and therefore should be kept accurate and deleted once no longer required. Many companies will take the view that as the Commissioner's primary role is to ensure that the data subjects are not harmed by the misuse of personal data, so long as the tapes are kept securely and the data on them is not merged with any live data without scrupulous checks that the Data Protection principles are being adhered to, the Commissioner is not likely to take action.

6. Processed in accordance with the data subject's rights;

This means that data must not be processed:

- if the data controller has not complied with the data subject's rights of access to personal data (under Section 7);
- if the data subject has objected to processing on the grounds that to carry on with the processing would cause damage or distress (under Section 10);
- if the data subject has objected to direct marketing (under Section 11);
- if the data controller is in breach of Section 13 (which allows the data subject to object to automated decision taking).

7. Secure

Personal data must be kept secure and protected from unauthorized access. This means that the data controller must not only take technical measures (like using password protected access) but also ensure that only suitable staff have access to it. The extent of the steps to be taken depends on the type of data and the likelihood of harm that may result (presumably to the data subject) from a security breach. You would be wise to put measures such as the following in place:

- limiting access to data through appropriate passwords, etc;
- limiting physical access to the disks and tapes on which the data is held;
- vetting staff who have access to the data;
- providing training in data security to staff who have access to the data;

- keeping backups of data to ensure it can be restored in case of loss or error;
- appropriate identification procedures to ensure that personal data are only disclosed to the appropriate people (for example, giving the data subjects a password or pass phrase to verify their identity);
- cross-checking the data to ensure accuracy (for example, removing multiple entries, checking addresses against postcode databases, and analysing the data to throw out badly-formed telephone numbers);
- having procedures in place to ensure that data are erased once they are no longer required;
- having a procedure to ensure regular updating of data (for example, telephoning data subjects on a rolling cycle to check their data are being kept up-to-date);
- reviewing on a regular basis all of the procedures in relation to the above to make sure they are still valid.

As part of the notification process, you are required to submit a brief statement of the steps you intend to take to comply with this principle. A good way to comply with both this obligation and the general obligation of this principle is to perform a risk assessment relating to the data and to modify internal processes accordingly.

There is a British Standard for information security, BS7799 (ISO17799), which the Information Commissioner has stated provides a suitable benchmark for compliance with this principle. However, BS7799 is a very comprehensive standard and it is not necessary to be fully compliant with BS7799 in order to comply with this principle. More information can be obtained from BSI or ISO.

'Proportionality' is a buzzword currently used a lot in the regulatory context: it simply means that the steps taken should be adequate but not excessive in relation to the likely harm which could be suffered arising from a breach. Clearly, an organization holding health records would have to take significantly greater security measures than an organization holding a mailing list of email addresses of people interested in gardening, for example.

Where you appoint a third party to undertake data processing for you (for example, a payroll bureau), you must take steps to ensure that they comply with similar obligations in relation to data security and you are required to have a written contract with them which imposes these obligations.

8. Not transferred to countries without adequate protection

It is unlawful to pass personal data to any country which does not have adequate protection for data subjects. This is a contentious and difficult topic, but the major points are as follows.

- All EEA countries are deemed to have adequate protection. When new countries join the EU it will therefore become lawful to transmit data to those countries.

- The US does not have adequate protection. However, the US Department of Commerce, in conjunction with the European Commission (EC), has set up a scheme called Safe Harbor (2000) which allows US businesses to sign up to a set of principles equivalent to those in the Data Protection Act and which therefore makes transfers of data to those companies legitimate.

- The EC periodically makes decisions (European Commission 1995) that various territories do have adequate levels of protection and that data can be passed there freely. At the time of writing, only Guernsey, Hungary, Switzerland, Argentina and (for certain purposes) the Canadian province of Quebec are deemed to have adequate levels of protection. It is likely that the Isle of Man will soon be added to the list.

- Irrespective of whether the country in question has an adequate level of protection, the data subject can give their consent to the transfer and the transfer may comply with certain other criteria (which can be found in Schedule 4 to the Act).

- The EU has produced a model contract (European Commission 2001) which, in effect, imposes obligations on recipients of personal data in countries outside the EU equivalent to those which exist in the EU. If an EU data controller enters into this model contract with a recipient outside the EU, then data transfer becomes legitimate.

- Transit of data through a country is not the same as transfer to a country. Internet traffic may pass through the US, for example, en route from the United Kingdom to Germany but this does not amount to a transfer within the meaning of the Act. The best view is probably that if anything amounting to 'processing' goes on in a country, then there is a transfer to that country, but otherwise the data is just in transit and there is no breach of this principle.

RIGHTS OF DATA SUBJECTS

In brief, data subjects have the right to have their data processed only in accordance with the data protection principles set out above, and:

- to receive information about the identity of the person processing their data, the purposes of the processing and any other relevant details (including details of the source, or classes of the source, of the data and the persons, or classes of persons, to whom such data may be disclosed);

- to receive a copy of the data which a data controller may hold on them;

- to object to automated decision-taking. The purpose of this is to protect data subjects against processes such as automated credit-scoring:

data subjects can require that a human being is actively involved in the decision-making process;

- to prevent their details being used for direct marketing purposes;
- to prevent processing likely to cause damage or distress;
- to have inaccurate data corrected or erased;
- to receive compensation for breaches of the Act;
- to have the Commissioner consider a request for assessment where the data subject believes that the data controller may not be carrying out processing in accordance with the Act.

The right to receive information about the data processor

For processing to be fair the data controller must provide information about who is processing the data and why they are processing it. They must also provide any other information which may in the circumstances be required to make the processing fair. This is why every company website should have a privacy policy setting out this information (almost any company website will involve an invitation to provide personal data to the company, even if it only consists of an email address for enquiries). The right to receive a copy of the data which the data controller holds is subject to a £10 maximum fee.

Complying with data subject access requests

You are obliged to provide a data subject with details of the data you hold on them. You should consider the following questions:

- Have they paid you a fee? You can set a fee for this, up to a maximum of £10.
- Is this their first request or have they requested before? If they have requested before, you are allowed to refuse a subsequent request before a 'reasonable interval' has elapsed (there is no guidance on what this means).
- Have they provided you with information about the data they are looking for? A request cannot be a fishing expedition through all of the data that you hold: you are entitled to be told what sort of data the subject is looking for; for example, mailing databases, accounts details, personnel records.
- Have they provided you with enough information so that you can be sure they are who they say they are (e.g. copy of driving licence and utility bill)?
- Is there any other exemption relating to the data or the application?

once you are satisfied with the answers to those questions, you can proceed to collate the information, bearing in mind that:

- you must withhold or make anonymous information that identifies another data subject, unless you have that data subject's consent. For example, if an employee asks for details of complaints about them, releasing the complaints may identify the complainants, in which case the data cannot generally be disclosed without the complainant's consent. Simply removing the complainant's name may not be sufficient, as the data subject may still be able to identify the complainant from the other contents of the complaint. In this case, you should decline the request, giving reasons. However, you can not use this as a blanket excuse to refuse disclosure, as you are under a positive obligation to try to make the data available to the requesting data subject if you can. Make sure a copy of your reasoning is retained, in case you are required to justify your decision to the Commissioner or the Court. The question of disclosure is tricky and you should take expert advice in all but the most clear-cut cases.

- the time limit for compliance with the request is 40 days from the day you receive the request, the day you get the fee or the day you get the information containing details of the data subject's identity, whichever is the latest.

- the data provided to the data subject should be in a clear format that can be read by the human eye.

EXEMPTIONS

The Data Protection Act is a complex piece of legislation with many exemptions from its main rules depending on the circumstances. In the main, the exemptions are:

- from notification;

- from providing information to the data subject about who you are and the reasons for processing their data (the 'Subject Information Provisions'); and

- from providing the data subject with copies of the information you hold about them (the 'Subject Access Provisions').

There is not scope in this book to go into the exemptions in any detail. However, it is worth bearing in mind that there are general exemptions from the provisions of the Act in relation to national security, detection and prosecution of crime, giving and receiving legal advice, domestic purposes and journalism, literature and art.

More specific exemptions apply in certain circumstances, such as where disclosing the information would affect the value of a company's stock or where there are ongoing negotiations affecting the data subject (e.g. a canny data subject cannot use the Data Protection Act to find out what pay award his employer is thinking of giving him).

PENALTIES AND ENFORCEMENT

The Information Commissioner has the primary responsibility for enforcement of the Act and the primary mechanism is by means of an Enforcement Notice. When the Information Commissioner believes that a data controller is contravening the Act, he may issue an Enforcement Notice which sets out steps which the data controller must take to bring the processing within the law. Failure to comply with it is a criminal offence (and managers and directors of an infringing company will also be liable). There are some other criminal offences contained in the Act:

- unlawful obtaining or disclosing of personal data;
- selling or offering to sell unlawfully-obtained personal data;
- enforced subject access.

This probably needs a little more explanation: it used to be a frequent practice for employers to require prospective employees to obtain a copy of their criminal record from the police prior to offering them employment. Clearly, the employer could not obtain this information directly but the employee could. It is now a criminal offence to require someone else to obtain personal data about themselves in connection with that person's work.

There are also some administrative offences which make it a crime to interfere with the work of the Information Commissioner or the administration or enforcement of the Act. It is, of course a crime to fail to notify, to provide false statements to the Information Commissioner, to fail to notify him of any changes to a notification and to fail to co-operate with him in certain circumstances.

REFERENCES

European Commission (1995) *Directive 95/46/EC, Article 25(6)*. Available at http://www.europa.eu.int/comm/internal_market/privacy/adequacy_en.htm.

European Commission (2001) *Model Contracts for the transfer of personal data to third countries*. Available at http://www.europa.eu.int/comm/internal_market/privacy/modelcontracts_en.htm.

Information Commissioner (2003) Comments on *Durant v. Financial Services Authority* [2003] EWCA Civ 1746. Available at http://ico-cms.amaze.co.uk/DocumentUploads/151203%20Durant.pdf.

US Department of Commerce (2000) *Safe Harbor*. Available at http://www.export.gov/safeharbor/sh_overview.html.

Reproduced by permission of Moorcrofts

10 Doing Business Electronically

JEREMY NEWTON

Law-makers around the world are trying to keep pace with rapid developments in ecommerce. This chapter does not aim to discuss all the initiatives in depth but it outlines the reasons for this activity and looks at some of the new laws and what they mean for business.

INTRODUCTION

The UK's first conference on internet law took place in 1995, when businesses were starting to get to grips with the legal issues of doing business electronically. A frequent comment at that point was that the internet was lawless – a kind of 'electronic frontier', where wrongdoers were protected both by the anonymity of cyberspace and the complexities of seeking legal remedies internationally. Early commentators took the view that the law would be hard-pushed to keep up with the development of ecommerce and the new problems to which it gave rise.

In fact, law-makers around the world have endeavoured strenuously to keep pace with the rapid developments in this field. In Europe, there have been numerous directives touching on various aspects of ecommerce (including the Electronic Commerce Directive, the Distance Selling Directive, the Electronic Signatures Directive and the Directive on Electronic Money Institutions), new regulations about determining jurisdiction for international contract disputes, new rules about distance marketing of financial services, new initiatives about VAT on products delivered electronically, and so on.

The European Commission's stated aims in the field of ecommerce law were set out in a 1997 Green Paper entitled 'A European Initiative in Electronic Commerce'. These aims included encouraging the vigorous growth of ecommerce in Europe, and the Commission noted that one of the impediments to Europe's ability to challenge the US in this arena was the lack of a suitable legal and institutional framework at EU level to support the new ecommerce technologies. A common framework was needed to help promote trust and confidence in the technologies, thus encouraging their take-up by businesses and consumers, and to bring down the barriers to cross-border trade that were being created by the various EU member states bringing into force different national ecommerce laws.

These two imperatives – promoting trust and confidence in ecommerce and facilitating cross-border trade within the single European market – lie behind much of the 'ecommerce law' that now has effect in the UK. Of the various European Directives mentioned above, most have now been implemented in English law by means of statutes or regulations and, against that background, this chapter will outline the following aspects of doing business electronically:

- the need for special authorizations;
- the information to be made available to clients;
- the rules about forming contracts electronically (e.g. by email or via a website);
- the regulations about the client's rights of cancellation;
- the determination of the applicable law if the service provider and the client are based in different countries;
- the rules concerning marketing or other commercial communications sent electronically;
- the implications of non-compliance with UK regulations;
- the treatment of VAT on products delivered electronically.

TERMINOLOGY

- Information society services: 'Any service normally provided for remuneration, at a distance, by means of electronic equipment for the processing ... and storage of data, and at the individual request of a recipient of the service'. This encompasses (amongst other things) advertising and selling goods by email or on websites, as well as network access or hosting activities. The Electronic Commerce Directive (and the Regulations which implement it in the UK) deals generally with the provision of information society services.

- Service provider: 'Any person who provides an information society service' – for example, a company that sells books over the internet.

- Service recipients and consumers: 'Any person who, for professional ends or otherwise, uses an information society service, in particular for the purposes of seeking information or making it accessible'. This includes both individuals and corporate bodies – for example, a bank which makes use of an online credit-rating service. By contrast, a 'consumer' is 'any natural person who is acting for purposes other than those of his trade, business or profession'. The significance of the distinction is that the law imposes more rigorous requirements on service providers in relation to their dealings with consumers than in relation to dealings with other businesses.

PRIOR AUTHORIZATION

To encourage online business, the Electronic Commerce Directive provided that the start of activity of an information society service provider should not be subject to any prior authorization requirements. In other words, no

EU member state may impose authorization schemes targeted specifically at the electronic provision of goods or services. This approach was intended to counter the risk of various EU member states imposing different requirements about setting up as an ecommerce operator.

However, any authorization schemes which are not specifically targeted at information society services continue to apply. Obvious examples are authorizations relating to the sale of alcohol, drugs or firearms. Businesses still need to comply with any national licensing requirements that apply to such products or services, irrespective whether they are selling them electronically or 'face to face'.

INFORMATION TO BE PROVIDED TO CLIENTS

One of the key aims of the Electronic Commerce Directive was to promote trust and confidence in ecommerce. One of the main ways to achieve this is by ensuring greater transparency about the identity of any service provider. The electronic environment can make it difficult for a client to tell exactly who he is contracting with and where they are established. So the Commission proposed that certain information requirements should be imposed on all ecommerce service providers in order to help promote trust in their identity. The Directive (and the UK Electronic Commerce (EC Directive) Regulations 2002) accordingly set out the information that a service provider must make available to service recipients.

Besides these general information requirements, however, the law imposes an additional set of requirements in relation to consumers entering into 'distance contracts'. These requirements arise mainly under the European Distance Selling Directive 1997 and have been incorporated into English law in the Consumer Protection (Distance Selling) Regulations 2000. These Regulations are not directed exclusively at information society service providers: they apply equally to businesses selling goods or services to consumers by mail order, telephone or fax.

There is a significant area of overlap between the information requirements set out in the Electronic Commerce Regulations and those of the Distance Selling Regulations. For ease of reference, a consolidated checklist of these requirements is set out in the Appendix. It should be stressed, though, that certain industries may be subject to additional legal requirements or codes of practice about the information that must be provided to clients.

Requirements under the Electronic Commerce (EC Directive) Regulations 2002

Service providers must make the following information available in a form that is 'easily, directly and permanently accessible' (inclusion of this information on a website should be sufficient to meet this requirement):

- name of the service provider;
- geographic address at which the service provider is established;
- contact details for the service provider (including email address) to enable direct and effective communication;
- details of any trade or similar register in which the service provider is registered, together with the registration number;
- details of any supervisory authority, where the provision of the service is subject to an authorization scheme;
- details of any professional body with which the service provider is registered and of how the applicable professional conduct rules may be accessed;
- VAT registration number.

The Regulations also require that any statements as to prices must be 'clear and unambiguous' and, in particular, must indicate whether they are inclusive of tax and delivery costs. Additional information requirements apply where contracts are to be formed electronically.

Requirements under the Consumer Protection (Distance Selling) Regulations 2000

Service providers must make the following information available in good time before the contract is made:

- the identity of the supplier and, where the contract requires payment in advance, the supplier's address;
- a description of the goods or services;
- the price of the goods or services (including all taxes);
- delivery costs where appropriate;
- arrangements for payment, delivery and performance;
- the existence of a right of cancellation;
- the costs of using the means of distance communication in question;
- the period for which the offer or price remains valid;
- where appropriate, the minimum duration of the contract (in cases where the supply of goods or services is to be on a permanent or recurrent basis).

The information must be given in a clear and comprehensible manner, in a form appropriate to the means of distance communications used and with due regard to principles of good faith. The supplier must also inform the consumer if it proposes to provide substitute goods or services if those ordered are unavailable and, if so, that the cost of returning such substitutes will be met by the supplier if the consumer chooses to cancel the contract.

The Distance Selling Regulations go on to stipulate certain additional information that must be supplied either prior to the formation of the contract or, at the latest, by the time that either the goods are delivered or the services are performed. This information has to be provided 'in writing or in another durable medium which is available and accessible to the consumer'. The general view is that an email containing this information should suffice, as the consumer can then decide whether to store the information electronically or to print it off. The additional information consists of:

- the identity of the supplier and, where the contract requires payment in advance, the supplier's address;
- a description of the goods or services;
- the price of the goods or services (including all taxes);
- delivery costs where appropriate;
- the arrangements for payment, delivery and performance;
- the existence of a right of cancellation and information about the relevant conditions, procedures and costs associated with cancellation;
- the geographical address of the supplier to which the consumer may address complaints;
- information about any after-sales services and guarantees.

It should be noted that failure to provide this additional information has implications for the enforceability of the contract, as the duration of the client's right to cancel a distance contract depends primarily on the date on which this information is provided.

FORMING CONTRACTS ELECTRONICALLY

Legal structure of a binding contract

The starting point for any explanation of online contract formation is to outline the legal concepts of 'offer and acceptance'. Under English law, the following elements must be present in order to create a legally-binding contract:

- an offer – an expression of willingness to enter into a contract on certain terms, made with the intention that a contract will exist once the offer is accepted;
- an acceptance – the unqualified assent to the terms of an offer;
- consideration – the element of value that each party gives the other under the contract (for example, the provision of goods by one party, in return for the payment of money by the other);
- an intention to create legally-binding relations (which the law normally takes for granted in commercial contexts).

This analysis of the elements of offer and acceptance is important for any business developing an online offering. The general rule is that a contract is formed when an offer has been accepted. But displaying products and prices in an electronic 'shop window' can amount to a unilateral offer which – if accepted – can create a legally-binding obligation on the part of the supplier to fulfil an unlimited number of orders on those terms. There have been numerous illustrations of retailers being caught out by this principle such as the Hoover Air Miles debacle in the late 1990s and, more recently, Argos inadvertently advertising £299 television sets on its website at a price of just £2.99, with thousands of orders being placed before the error was noticed.

For this reason, it is important to ensure that offerings on a website are structured not as 'offers', but rather as 'invitations to treat'. In other words, the website does nothing more than invite offers from potential clients to purchase at the stated price, with the supplier then free to accept or reject the offer as it sees fit. The website should also state that no contract is formed unless and until the supplier has notified the client that it accepts the order.

Other legal formalities

In terms of the formalities applicable to electronic contracts, there used to be significant differences between the requirements of the various EU member states. Just as different national authorization schemes for service providers tended to create barriers to trade within the EU, so differing national laws about contract formation could create uncertainty about the validity and enforceability of contracts formed electronically.

The Electronic Commerce Directive required all member states to ensure that their national law allows contracts to be concluded by electronic means and recognizes the legal effectiveness of agreements formed in this way. (This was not really in doubt in the UK, but other member states have had to get to grips with new and very different rules about the form of a contract in light of the Directive.)

There are some predictable exceptions to this general rule – for example, contracts for the sale of land or those governed by family law – but the law is clear that the majority of commercial agreements can now be formed electronically and that electronic contracts should be upheld by the courts. The Directive (and the UK Electronic Commerce Regulations) go on to stipulate the information to be provided by service providers where contracts are concluded in this way.

Besides the general information requirements set out above, if a contract is to be concluded by electronic means, the service provider must provide the following additional information in a clear, comprehensible and unambiguous manner before the order is placed by the service recipient:

- the technical steps required to form the contract – for example 'Click to confirm order' – so that the service recipient understands at exactly what point in the process he becomes legally committed to the contract;

- the technical means for identifying and correcting input errors prior to placing of the order;

- the languages offered for the conclusion of the contract;

- any relevant codes of conduct to which the service provider subscribes and how these can be consulted electronically;

- whether or not the contract will be 'filed' by the service provider – a legal concept that is primarily relevant to non-UK service providers and so is not dealt with further here – and, if so, how it can be accessed.

Orders placed through technological means must generally be acknowledged 'without undue delay' and by electronic means. (The requirements above do not apply, however, where contracts are concluded by the exchange of individual emails.) Any contractual terms and conditions provided by the service provider must also be made available in a manner that enables the service recipient to store and reproduce them.

PERFORMANCE AND CANCELLATION

As a further measure to protect consumers, the Distance Selling Directive requires member states to introduce time limits for the performance of contracts by the supplier and to establish a right for the consumer to cancel the distance contract within specified time limits.

With regard to performance, the general rule is that the supplier must perform the contract within 30 days from the day following the date of the client's order (though the parties can agree otherwise). If the supplier cannot perform the contract within that period, it must inform the consumer and reimburse any sum paid, unless the contract provided for the supply of alternative goods or services.

With regard to cancellation, the Distance Selling Regulations contain detailed provisions describing how and when the cancellation right can be invoked and the arrangements for reimbursement and the return of any products supplied. A detailed discussion of these is beyond the scope of this chapter, but the major point to note is in relation to the timing of the cancellation period. The cancellation period begins on the date of the contract and ends on a date determined as follows:

- if the supplier has complied properly with all the 'additional information requirements', the cancellation period ends seven working days after the consumer receives the goods (or after the date of the contract for services);

- if the supplier has not complied with those requirements, but provides the additional information (in writing or another durable medium) within three months of the contract date, the cancellation period ends seven days after the consumer receives the information;

- if neither of the above applies, then the cancellation period ends three months and seven working days after the consumer receives the goods (or the contract for services is concluded).

There are a few predictable exceptions to this cancellation right – for example, contracts for the supply of goods which are likely to deteriorate rapidly, contracts where the price of the goods is subject to financial fluctuations, contracts for audio or video recordings which have been unsealed and contracts for newspapers or magazines – but most distance contracts with consumers do now carry this statutory cancellation right. Businesses selling their goods and services electronically must therefore ensure that their staff have a thorough understanding of the cancellation rules and time limits, in order to minimize the risk of legal complaints by dissatisfied clients.

JURISDICTION

Regardless of the legality of an electronic contract, doing business across national boundaries inevitably raises questions as to whose laws apply and in which country one party may sue another. For example, Yahoo! was ordered (by a French court) to block French users from viewing an online auction of Nazi memorabilia. The website in question was hosted in the US (and Yahoo! is, of course, a US company), but the French court decided that it had jurisdiction to rule on the application of the French law prohibiting the display of Nazi symbols.

Operating as an information society service provider

The law relating to these issues is somewhat convoluted but, in the context of ecommerce, the main rules can be found in the Electronic Commerce Directive and in the UK Electronic Commerce Regulations, which regulate the principles applicable in what is called the 'coordinated field' (i.e. the set of requirements that relate to information society services or service providers, concerning the taking up and pursuit of the activity of an information society service – for example, requirements relating to authorizations or to contracting).

Under the Regulations, service providers established in the UK – whether they are selling only into the UK or also overseas – must comply with any requirements within the coordinated field. UK enforcement authorities (like the Director-General of Fair Trading) are responsible for ensuring compliance by UK service providers but have no such responsibility with regard to service providers in other member states. By the same token, the equivalent legislation in other member states means that their national enforcement authorities can take action against businesses established in their respective countries in relation to the coordinated field, but not against UK businesses. This has become commonly known as the 'Country of Origin Principle' or 'Home State Regulation'.

It is important to understand the limits of this country of origin principle. It does not mean that a UK service provider is under no obligation to comply with non-UK laws. The coordinated field does not include, for example, requirements applicable to goods, so suppliers still have to be sensitive to differing national rules about quality, labelling and promotional arrangements. The Regulations are also stated not to apply to matters such data protection, competition law, gambling and taxation.

For companies looking to sell goods or services into non-UK markets, then, it remains as important as ever to understand the legal requirements of those overseas jurisdictions about the particular products on offer and the manner in which transactions are handled.

Consumer contracts

In terms of jurisdiction – that is, which courts can hear a dispute – the Brussels Convention provides that, in the event of a dispute based on a contract between an EU supplier and an EU consumer, the consumer will generally be able to go to his own courts to sue the supplier – or to put it another way, the business 'plays away' in most cases. Any judgment given by the consumer's 'home' court would be enforceable through the courts in the supplier's jurisdiction. The other side of that coin is that a business which wants to sue a consumer also needs to do so in the consumer's own state. (A few non-EU countries – Iceland, Lichtenstein, Norway and Switzerland – are also covered by the Regulation and Denmark, an EU member, opted-out of the Regulation.)

A website is only caught by the Regulation if it is 'directing' its activities at the relevant states. There is little legal guidance on what that actually means but a site is likely to be covered if it fulfils orders to consumers in a particular state or uses a particular state's language or currency for promoting its products.

The problem this poses for businesses is how to protect themselves against being sued in all the different territories. Businesses dealing in consumer products or services should include terms on the website clearly indicating its target markets and should ideally block orders from purchasers with a physical delivery address in other states.

Business to business contracts

Different rules apply in relation to business to business contracts, where the parties can generally exclude the operation of overseas laws and jurisdiction by clearly making the contract subject to the jurisdiction of the English courts.

MARKETING COMMUNICATIONS

The Electronic Commerce Directive (and the UK Electronic Commerce Regulations) set out strict rules as to how businesses go about marketing themselves electronically. These rules apply to a broad category of 'commercial communications' – practically any communication, in any form, designed to promote the goods, services or image of a business.

It is the responsibility of the service provider to ensure that any commercial communication provided by him in connection with an information society service:

- is clearly identifiable as a commercial communication;
- clearly identifies the person on whose behalf the commercial communication is made;
- clearly identifies as such any promotional offers or competitions, together with any related conditions.

The Regulations also set out special rules for unsolicited commercial communications sent by email (i.e. spam). These must be 'clearly and unambiguously identifiable as such as soon as they are received' – the rationale being to give the recipient the opportunity to delete them immediately without troubling to open them. In fact, this requirement has been reinforced by later rules under the Privacy and Electronic Communications (EC Directive) Regulations 2003, which ban the sending of unsolicited emails without the prior consent of the recipient. Data protection compliance is an important consideration for any provider of information society services and is discussed further in Chapter 9.

CONSEQUENCES OF NON-COMPLIANCE

The consequences of non-compliance with the Electronic Commerce Regulations and the Distance Selling Regulations can be serious. The implications of non-compliance with the information requirements in the Distance Selling Regulations, in terms of a consumer's rights to cancel the contract, have been outlined above.

The consumer protection aspects of the Distance Selling Regulations and the Electronic Commerce Regulations are also enforceable by authorities such as the Office of Fair Trading or local trading standards offices, who can apply a 'Stop Now Order' from the courts, requiring the service provider to cease any breach of the Regulations which harms the collective interest of consumers. Failure to comply with a Stop Now Order can ultimately result in a fine or imprisonment.

Leaving aside consumer protection specifically, the Electronic Commerce Regulations also provide:

- that the service provider's duties with regard to the information requirements and the provisions about commercial communications are enforceable by clients by means of an action for damages for breach of statutory duty;
- that failure to provide a copy of contract terms and conditions may give rise to the client seeking a court order requiring the service provider to comply;

- that failure to provide the means for a client to identify and correct input errors at the time of placing an order results in the client having the unilateral right to rescind the contract.

VAT ISSUES

Changes in the VAT treatment of ecommerce transactions mean that businesses need to be aware of the regime that came into force in July 2003. In order to understand the new rules, it is helpful to consider the earlier position.

VAT before July 2003

Most ecommerce transactions were taxed under the rule that the place of supply for services is the place where the supplier is located (unless otherwise provided). In practical terms this meant:

- Where an EU-based supplier sold to an EU consumer or to a consumer outside the EU, it had to charge VAT at the rate applicable where the supplier is based.
- Where a non-EU supplier sold to an EU business, VAT was paid by the importing company under self-supply arrangements, at the rate applicable where the importer was based.
- Where a non-EU supplier sold to an EU private consumer however, it had no obligation to charge VAT at all.

VAT since July 2003

These rules were viewed as putting EU traders at a competitive disadvantage when selling to private consumers, and new rules are now in force which allow for the VAT registration of foreign ecommerce traders and the distribution of VAT receipts to the member states where the services were used. The new rules apply to products such as downloaded software, downloaded text, information or images (including making databases available) and digitized publications.

Location of Supplier	Type of Client	Tax rule
Outside the EU	EU business	VAT-registered businesses pay VAT under self-assessment arrangements.
Outside the EU	EU private client	The supplier has to register with a VAT authority in an EU member state and levies VAT at the rate applicable in the member state where the client is resident (i.e. the supplier will charge different VAT rates depending on the place of taxation within the EU). The VAT rate applicable is the same as that for a business buyer in the same member state as the client. The country of registration re-allocates the VAT revenue to the country of the consumer. The non-EU business will have a simpler registration requirement than EU traders and non-EU businesses generally. The registration model can be completed online without need for a fiscal representative or for any physical presence. However, the varying rates of VAT will increase the ongoing administrative burden.
EU	Non-EU	Place of taxation is where client is located – not subject to VAT.
EU	EU business	Place of supply is where the business client is located.
EU	EU private client	Place of supply is where the supplier is located.

OTHER CONSIDERATIONS

It is clear that the law relating to ecommerce and doing business online is changing rapidly and dramatically. This chapter has discussed the rules that are likely to be relevant to businesses generally but has not endeavoured to address any of the issues specific to individual sectors (for example, there are completely separate regulations on the distance marketing of financial services) or to businesses operating as intermediary service providers or ISPs (the Electronic Commerce Directive deals at length with the liabilities of ISPs in respect of content which they 'host' or 'cache' or for which they are otherwise a conduit). Nor has it touched on some of the more advanced considerations for the service provider, such as the use of electronic signatures.

However, there are numerous other sources of information for any company seeking to establish online operations:

- The Department of Trade and Industry (DTI) provides guidance about distance selling and ecommerce and its website includes links to the UK Regulations.

- The Office of Fair Trading (OFT) website includes information for businesses about consumer protection, including Stop Now Orders.

- The Office of the Information Commissioner provides guidance about the collection and use of client data in the context of ecommerce operations.

APPENDIX: CONSOLIDATED INFORMATION REQUIREMENTS

Information to be provided by all service providers

- Name and geographic address
- Contact details for the service provider (including email) to enable direct and effective communication
- Details of any trade or similar register in which the service provider is registered, together with the registration number
- Details of any supervisory authority, where the provision of the service is subject to an authorization scheme
- Details of any professional body with which the service provider is registered and of how the applicable professional conduct rules may be accessed
- VAT registration number

Note that all price indications must be 'clear and unambiguous' and must indicate whether they are inclusive of tax and delivery costs.

Additional pre-contract information to be provided to consumers

- Description of the goods or services
- Arrangements for payment, delivery and performance
- Existence of a right of cancellation
- Costs (if any) of using the means of distance communication
- Period for which the offer or price remains valid
- Where appropriate, the minimum duration of the contract (in cases where the supply of goods or services is to be on a permanent or recurrent basis)
- Whether the supplier proposes to provide substitute goods or services (if those ordered are unavailable) and, if so, that the cost of returning such substitutes will be met by the supplier if the consumer chooses to cancel the contract

Additional post-contract information to be provided to consumers

- The existence of a right of cancellation
- Information about the relevant conditions, procedures and costs associated with cancellation
- The geographical address of the supplier to which the consumer may address complaints
- Information about any after-sales services and guarantees

11 Setting up Joint Ventures

ANDREW KATZ

A joint venture is an increasingly popular way of doing business, especially in the high-tech arena. This chapter discusses the issues that you should consider when embarking upon a joint venture.

INTRODUCTION

A 'joint venture' is not a fixed legal term: it covers a multitude of different business structures, from straightforward channel-to-market arrangements (like agency and distribution) to collaborative partnerships between two or more parties, which may include the formation of a new business, complete with its own staff, premises, branding, products, supply chain, etc.

What all joint ventures have in common is that each party believes it is offering something complementary to the other parties. In combination, the joint venture is greater than the contributions of the individual parties. Most joint ventures also have an element of sharing risk as well as sharing the reward (something which brings its own legal problems).

Perhaps the biggest mistake the joint venture parties can make is to concentrate on the mechanism of setting up the joint venture, without giving sufficient thought both to how the joint venture is to be run on a day-to-day basis and to how the parties are to exit from the arrangement. In terms of day-to-day management, the question is really one of managing expectations: most joint venture documents give extensive thought to the amount of financial commitment that each partner will put into the project. Fewer, however, take time to think in terms of the non-financial input, particularly manpower. Even fewer joint venture documents adequately address the question of exit. Is one joint venture partner to be given an option to purchase the other? Is the entire joint venture to be sold as a going concern (and if so, will it still require any input from the former partners)? To maximize the success of a joint venture, the parties need to address those questions.

JOINT VENTURES AND IT PROJECTS

Perhaps the most compelling reason why joint ventures have been popular in the technology market is that they are perceived to be a quick way of getting a business up and running without a large cash commitment. Almost always, it is theoretically possible for a joint venture partner to buy in the skills it needs, if the cash is available. However, it may be more effective for a cash-strapped start-up to obtain that resource in exchange for a share in the rewards, rather than having to reach into its pocket and fund it. Much of the resource required may have a low marginal cost to the supplier, when provided to the joint venture, but would be much more expensive to purchase on the open market.

CASE STUDY

New.com wishes to offer a transaction-based service on the internet. Rather than purchasing both the computer hardware and the software it requires on the open market, it sees a joint venture relationship with the supplier of the software and with an internet hosting company as a low-risk and low-cost means of bootstrapping the resources needed to run the project.

The software company's cost is little more than running off a copy of its software on CD and the internet service provider can (at least initially) provide some disk space and bandwidth for the project which may not have been used in any event. They are supplying resources at low marginal cost to themselves, in circumstances where they would probably not have made a cash sale to New.com in any event. For them, there is little initial risk, investment or effort, coupled with large potential gains if the project takes off.

Care has to be taken in managing the expectations of New.com and the other partners. For example, can the joint venture expect the same level of support and attentiveness from the software company as its fee-paying clients? Will New.com become resentful of the other two partners when the venture becomes successful and it realizes that its profits would have been much greater if it had bought the software and hosting for cash on the open market?

Occasionally, a joint venture is the only way forward in a relationship where a party has unique assets (for example, intellectual property such as patents or software) which it is unwilling to transfer or license directly to the other party. That partner may feel more comfortable where the licence is granted to a third party over which it has some control, rather than on arms' length terms.

Frequently, the sales staff of the joint venture partners can be used to cross-sell each other's products, thus giving bigger market penetration and the benefit that the names of the joint venture partners themselves will add credibility to the joint venture project.

ESTABLISHING A JOINT VENTURE

Non-disclosure agreements

Potential joint venture partners will necessarily spend some time finding out about each others' businesses and plans before committing to final documentation. This will frequently involve the parties disclosing sensitive information and, before any of this information is disclosed, all parties should have entered into a non-disclosure agreement (NDA). As disclosures may involve patentable inventions, failure to enter into an effective NDA could affect the validity of any later applications for patents. As well as covering secrecy, an NDA can cover areas such as non-poaching of staff during and after the negotiations and ownership of intellectual property created during negotiations. The parties' lawyers can advise on the terms of a suitable NDA.

Heads of agreement

The heads of agreement (or heads of terms) document sets out the commercial terms on which the joint venture will operate, in less legalistic terms than the full documentation, but nevertheless covering all the commercial bases of the deal. The key here is to negotiate the heads quickly, so that the parties do not end up negotiating the same points twice. The heads are not legally binding (in lawyers' jargon they are 'subject to contract' and the lawyers will ensure that they contain wording that expresses this properly). Even so, it is difficult for a party to change its mind on a point once it has been enshrined in the heads. A few points follow on from this:

- Establish what is legally binding and what is not as soon as possible. It is possible for parties to create a contract by exchange of letters alone. To avoid this happening, ensure that all correspondence involving joint venture negotiations is marked 'subject to contract', until the final documentation is ready to be signed.

- Do not start operating the joint venture until you have final, signed documentation. If you do so, you could be deemed to have entered into a contract with your joint venture partner on terms that only a court case will be able to unravel.

- Establish who is going to pay the professional advisers' costs, whether or not the joint venture goes ahead.

Many joint venture negotiations end up nowhere, but that is likely to be lot better than a failed joint venture for all parties, in terms of cost, loss of management time and market perception. The heads of agreement document allows the parties to reach a red or green light as quickly as possible before too much money and management time have been wasted.

Managing expectations – the business plan

For a successful joint venture, the involvement of each party needs to be explicitly stated as soon as possible. A software supplier in a joint venture with a hardware supplier may assume that its products are going to be sold by a hardware supplier's sales staff and that the products will be co-branded, but unless this is explicitly stated at the outset, the hardware supplier may turn out to have different expectations. To argue 'we will both make more money that way' is never quite as simple as it seems and the perceptions of the partners must coincide. The documentation setting up the joint venture must address these issues explicitly.

The business plan is a critical document in articulating the joint aims and aspirations of the parties. A plan for regular review and updating of the business plan is vital in that disagreements arising out of the business plan can be dealt with before they grow into larger operational issues. Unstated assumptions tend to lead to disputes and a comprehensive business plan can usually weed out erroneous assumptions ('What do you mean you've put in a £2000 monthly licence fee for the supply of your software – you're supplying it for free, aren't you?').

Day-to-day management

The partners need to consider how the joint venture will run on a day-to-day basis. It may seem to be micromanagement to think about things like the design of the letterheads or who will sign off stationery expenses, but it is at this level where real disagreements can surface (as anyone who has ever sat in a board meeting or partners' meeting can testify).

Transpose your own experiences onto the joint venture: think about the processes you are familiar with in your own business and use them as a basis for setting up the business processes in the joint venture. If you have an operations handbook for your own business, use that as a starting point and try to develop a similar handbook for the joint venture. If you do this in conjunction with the other partners then you should end up with a workable model for day-to-day management which has flushed out potential disagreement. This will not be a simple or straightforward process, but working together on the handbook and the business plan will give each partner an invaluable feel for the style and culture of the joint venture.

As an aside, do not fall into the trap of believing that, because you have invested significant time and cost in investigating and negotiating a joint venture, you are obliged to enter into it. If, as part of the process of working together on setting it up, you become sure that you and the other partners cannot work together, walk away.

Ownership of intellectual property

Joint ventures frequently involve the development of intellectual property (IP). The parties may collaborate to develop new software, for example based on the software of one of the parties or linking the hardware of one party with the software of another. Generally, the IP will belong to the joint venture, but the parties need to address whether the partners are allowed access to it for their own purposes and, if so, on what terms and what happens to the IP in the joint venture exit arrangements.

Commonly, the joint venture will grant a royalty-free licence on the IP to the partners. If the joint venture folds, rather than have a squabble over who gets the IP, a sensible route is to put in place a mechanism whereby the IP can be exploited by each of the partners as if each partner owned it. Any subsequent developments belong solely to the partners who made them (this is known in the software business as 'forking'). The mechanism for achieving this can be a little complicated, but it is often the fairest way to proceed.

Exit arrangements

Joint ventures rarely last for ever and the partners should have a view as to how the joint venture is to end. Is the business secure enough to be sold on the open market? Can one party buy out the other? For example, if a channel-to-market joint venture establishes a bridgehead into a new jurisdiction, the supplying party is increasingly likely to want to purchase the joint venture to bring it into the group structure, in which case there should be an explicit mechanism for this to happen at an appropriate price.

This is part of the management of expectations: are the partners expecting a capital gain on exit within a defined period or a flow of profits from the venture? The exit aspirations of the venture need to be articulated, because a venture in which one partner is keen on maximizing short-term profits and the other demands constant re-investment with a view to growing the joint venture for eventual trade-sale is heading for disaster. Joint ventures in which the partners are at loggerheads are likely to decline and fail very quickly, both because they are unlikely to have management teams which are sufficiently independent (or have the inclination) to steer the venture away from trouble and because the partners are likely to be providing non-cash benefits to the venture which can easily be withdrawn in the event a dispute arises.

If the exit aspirations involve a sale of the joint venture company (or if there are plans for raising external finance), then the joint venture company has to be groomed for an inevitable due diligence process, and the partners' involvement in the joint venture company may have to be placed on a more arms' length basis than was probably the case when the joint venture was established.

The joint venture may be so intertwined with the business of one or more of the partners that it cannot effectively stand alone; in those circumstances the venture has to be viewed as an income-only rather than a capital growth proposition and an orderly wind-down needs to be planned for when the joint venture comes to an end.

STRUCTURE OF A JOINT VENTURE

Having decided on the aims of the joint venture, the partners need to settle on the most appropriate structure. At its simplest, the joint venture may consist of co-operative channel-to-market arrangements. A simple channel-to-market joint venture is characterized by a fairly straightforward distribution or agency arrangement, possibly with some additional items bolted on. For example, there is likely to be a trade mark licence which permits the agent/distributor to use the principal/supplier's trade marks. The principal/supplier may also provide additional resource, in terms of, for example, office space, software, consultancy or administration.

Distribution and agency agreements

What lawyers call a 'distribution agreement' is probably better known as a reseller agreement. The supplier sells the goods to the distributor; the distributor becomes the owner of the goods and pays the supplier for them. The distributor then sells the goods on to its client. In this case, there are two separate sales involved: the supplier to the distributor and the distributor to the client.

In contrast, an agency relationship involves an agent appointed by the principal to find clients. The agent may then pass details of the client back to the principal who can conclude the deal or the agent can be granted power to sign on the principal's behalf and conclude the deal for the principal. In each case, the agreement will set out precise limits of the power involved.

A distributor makes his money by selling at a higher price than that at which he purchases. An agent makes his money by receiving a commission on the sales that he makes. Where goods are being sold, the relationship is pretty straightforward. For services (including software), the distinction is more unclear. Legal theory lags somewhat behind what happens in practice and, although there is a billion-dollar industry in reselling shrink-wrapped software, lawyers are still pretty much at loggerheads as to what happens as a matter of legal theory. When dealing with services, the lawyers drafting the documents defining the relationship must take extra care as there are some important legal distinctions between the two models (in terms of liability, regulation and termination).

Both agency and distribution models can form the basis of a simple joint venture relationship, frequently where the supplier (or principal) wishes to use the distributor (or agent) to break into a new market.

Licensing and royalty deals

Licensing deals are very common in IT and are another form of a simple channel-to-market joint venture arrangement. Where a channel-to-market deal involves licensing it usually either echoes a reseller model (the owner sells software to the reseller which then sells it to the client, taking a cut in the process) or a royalty model (the owner permits the reseller to duplicate and sell copies of the software, remitting to the owner a percentage of its revenues as royalties). The former route tends to be used for shrink-wrapped software and the latter for OEM or component software.

'Bolt on' terms

Whenever any of these forms of channel-to-market arrangements is employed, there may well be additional duties and obligations placed on each party which deepen the relationship and make it more of a joint venture. On the part of the owner, additional obligations are likely to be:

- provision of training;
- provision of marketing support;
- permission to use the owner's names/logos;
- provision of front-line or second-line support to the reseller or its clients;
- provision of updates to the software;
- financial support for marketing;
- protection of its intellectual property for the benefit of the reseller.

On the part of the reseller, typical obligations are likely to be:

- sales targets;
- staffing requirements;
- provision of front-line support to clients;
- localization of products to local markets;
- provision of marketing information back to the owner and/or other resellers;
- protection of the owner's intellectual property.

Financially, the parties may be tempted to structure the deal so that they set up a new accounting ledger for the venture (without setting up a new company or other legal entity) into which they invest certain sums and then split the profits in a certain ratio. This has the danger that the relationship legally forms a partnership, with some unfortunate consequences.

Distribution and agency need not involve the creation of a new legal entity. Other forms of joint venture usually do. For this reason, and also for reasons of increased flexibility, more transparent exit arrangements and ease of introduction of new players, a large number of joint ventures involve the establishment of a new legal entity to undertake the joint venture activity.

WHEN IS A PARTNERSHIP NOT A PARTNERSHIP?

Lawyers tend to be much more precise about the way in which they use various terms than businesses do. For example, 'partnership' has a very strictly defined meaning at law, whereas many companies will refer to their 'partners' in a much looser sense. This can lead to problems.

In summary, where the parties are sharing risk as well as reward, there is always a danger that they will be regarded as 'partners' in the eyes of the law (even if the contract between them states that they are not). This has some undesirable consequences, one of which is that each partner becomes liable to the other for any losses of the partnership (and can bind the other in contracts). Another is that they become intertwined with each other for tax purposes (they may be required to file a separate partnership tax return, for example). A partnership agreement is the classic way of dealing with these issues.

Partnership agreements

In England and Wales, partnerships are governed by the Partnership Act 1890 (despite its age, this is still the current legislation). A huge number of businesses, including almost all solicitors and a very large number of accountants and other professional practices are run under partnership agreements. A partnership under the Act consists of a number of partners (individuals or companies) who have come together for a common business aim (with a view to making a profit). The liability of the partners is unlimited, meaning that if the partnership incurs losses, each partner is individually liable for, potentially, all of those losses. Partners agree the proportions in which they share any profits of the venture and also the proportions in which any losses are to be borne. Any business relationship having these characteristics is a partnership (whether the partners like it or not). The burden of unlimited liability is often enough to frighten off partners from using this structure. It is possible, however, to have a complex structure where each of the partners will form a limited company which becomes a partner. This way, the partners can benefit from the limited liability afforded by using a limited company. Partnerships do not have to publish their accounts.

Limited partnerships

There is another structure called a 'limited partnership' which is basically the same as a partnership, but with some sleeping partners who are not allowed to get involved in the business of the partnership and are allowed to limit their liability. The active partners still retain unlimited liability. Limited partnerships have to be registered at Companies House. They are rare: do not confuse them with limited liability partnerships which are a totally different animal with a confusingly similar name.

LEGAL PERSONS

Limited companies, limited liability partnerships and European economic interest groupings are example of 'Legal Persons', meaning that they have a legal existence independently of their directors or members. They can enter into contracts in their own name, they can sue and be sued, they can commit criminal offences. In fact, in the eyes of the law, they can do almost anything that a natural person (generally described as an 'individual' by lawyers) can do. Of course, they always need the intervention of an individual as an agent (such as a director) to make that legal relationship, but when acting in a company's name, a director is not also acting as an individual. If a director signs a contract on behalf of the company, it is the company that is liable, not the director. This is in contrast to partnerships, which (in English Law, but not in Scots Law) have no separate legal personality. A partner signing a contract on behalf of the partnership is always personally liable for the contract, as are the other partners. If all the directors and shareholders of a company die in a plane crash, the company continues to exist. If any partner in a partnership dies, the partnership ceases to exist, unless the remaining partners agree otherwise.

Limited liability partnerships

A limited liability partnership (LLP) is in effect a hybrid of a partnership and a limited company. It is a concept new to English Law. Like a limited company, it is a legal person and its existence is independent of its partners – called members. The members are insulated from the debts and liabilities of the partnership in much the same way as shareholders are in a limited company.

LLPs are new to English Law and tax advisers are quite excited about the possibilities they offer for tax planning (they are 'transparent' for tax purposes, meaning they are not taxable themselves, but are taxed through their members). Members can be other corporate bodies (e.g. limited companies or other LLPs, as well as individuals). In exchange for receiving limited liability status, LLPs, like limited companies, have to publish certain information, such as their accounts, at Companies House.

LLPs are likely to become more and more popular as vehicles for joint ventures. One potential drawback is the need to set out what the parties each receive from the LLP by way of profits.

Limited companies

Limited companies are legal persons that consist of shareholders, who own the company, and directors, who undertake its day-to-day management. Shareholders have no right to get involved in the day-to-day running of the company, a right which is entrusted to the directors. The shareholders' control of a company is ultimately enshrined in their power to remove and appoint directors. There is (usually) nothing stopping a director from also being a shareholder of the company. Normally, the shareholders' liability to the company is limited, in that a shareholder cannot be held liable for the debt or other liabilities of the company. A director is liable for any defaults as a director but, as a shareholder, the liability is (almost always) limited. Of course, a shareholder may lose the value of any shares held if the company folds.

Limited liability is very attractive to companies which want to join forces in an untried area. The parties form a company in which they each hold shares to carry out the venture. If the venture folds and the company fails, the parent companies will (in most normal circumstances) be insulated from any losses in the joint venture company (although parties dealing with the venture will be aware of this and may try to protect their interests by entering into a parent company guarantee).

Lawyers are very familiar with the limited company as a vehicle for joint ventures and will automatically think of it as an appropriate structure. The checklist set out in the Appendix assumes that a limited company is the appropriate vehicle, although the issues will also translate to the other entities.

Other structures

The structures described above all arise under English Law (the law of England and Wales). Other jurisdictions have more or less comparable structures. When the joint venture crosses jurisdictions, always consider which jurisdiction is appropriate for forming the joint venture vehicle. For example, Limited Liability Corporations in the United States (especially the Delaware LLC) offer flexibility of structure and scope for tax planning.

A European economic interest grouping (EEIG) is a creation of the EU. It is broadly similar to a partnership in that an EEIG has partners (at least two of which must be from different member states in the EU), who have joint and several liability and whose liability is unlimited. Unlike a partnership, the EEIG is a legal person. Like a partnership, it is transparent for tax. As an organization designed to be non-profit making (although profits are not prohibited), it is perhaps more suited to joint ventures aimed at research

FACTORS TO CONSIDER WHEN FORMING AN ENTITY

	Informal channel-to-market structure	Partnership	Limited company	Limited liability partnership
Taxation	Uncertain	Transparent (but must file partnership return)	Taxed as entity in own right	Transparent (but must file partnership return)
Third-party liability assumed by partners	Unlimited, especially if the venture is deemed to be a partnership	Partners are jointly and severally liable	Partners normally protected by limited liability	Partners normally protected by limited liability
Complexity	Simple	Reasonably simple	Moderate to complex	Moderate to complex
Certainty	Good, unless the venture deemed to be a partnership	Good	Good	Moderate (the structure is too new for total certainty)
International recognition	Good	Moderate	Good	Good (but new)
Ease of exit	Difficult to unbundle	Moderate (can sell business and/or underlying assets, but partners may retain some liabilities)	Good (can sell shares and/or underlying business)	Good (can sell partnership interests or underlying business)
Finances made public	No	No	Yes	Yes
Identity of partners made public	No (except in certain cases related to competition law)	Yes	Yes	Yes
Separate audit requirement	No	Not generally	Yes (above thresholds)	Yes (above thresholds)

and development rather than to profit-making channel-to-market joint ventures. To put EEIGs into perspective, by April 2002 Companies House in the UK had accepted registration of only 190 EEIGs since the legislation was introduced in 1989.

There are other UK structures such as companies limited by guarantee, unlimited companies, friendly, industrial and provident societies, and companies incorporated by Royal Charter. They may all to a greater or lesser extent be involved in joint venture activity, but their uses are very specialized and are not covered here.

THE OPERATING AGREEMENT

All joint ventures should have some sort of operating agreement which sets out the main facets of the relationship. What should be covered is dealt with in greater depth in the checklist in the Appendix.

The names and, to a certain extent, the structure of the various documents comprising the operating agreements will vary depending on the type of joint venture. For example, where a joint venture is formed using a limited company as the vehicle, the core documents will be the articles of association of the company coupled with a shareholders' agreement. There may be separate licence agreements (for the provision of intellectual property to the joint venture), management agreements (for the provision of specific management services by the joint venture partners) and property licences or leases (if one or more of the joint venture partners is providing space for the joint venture at their premises). For a partnership, the core document will be the partnership agreement. However, whatever structure is finally adopted, the fundamental issues which need to be adopted in the agreements are largely the same.

COMPETITION LAW

Whenever businesses start to collaborate, there may be a suspicion that they are no longer competing with each other, and as a result, any form of joint venture may fall foul of competition law.

Competition law is very complex, and this book has space for no more than the briefest summary. Within the UK, competition law is enshrined, in the main, in the Competition Act 1998. Within the context of the EU, competition law is based on Articles 81 and 82 of the Treaty of Rome. European and UK law are to a large extent harmonized, in that the 1998 Act was based on the European legislation and there is a strong interrelationship between the two.

UK competition law is concerned with activity which tends to restrict or distort competition within the UK, and European competition law is concerned with activity tending to restrict competition between European member states. International joint ventures may also be subject to the competition law (sometimes called 'anti trust' law) of other jurisdictions – notably the US.

Competition law is based on the premise that competition between businesses is a good thing and that if businesses get together to act in concert (such as forming a cartel), they not only decrease competition by effectively substituting one composite business where there were previously two, but the more powerful composite business can dictate terms to the market. On the other hand, it also recognizes that when small and medium businesses get together, they can combine to provide a more competitive force in the marketplace by competing with the larger players in that market. Competition law is therefore aimed at prohibiting activity which has an anti-competitive effect – such as businesses with large market shares combining to dominate the market – while encouraging activity which (broadly) allows smaller businesses to combine forces to compete with the bigger players.

This means that there is activity which is (almost) always absolutely prohibited by competition law (such as price fixing) and activity which is prohibited unless it is deemed sufficiently low-level not to affect the market. Low-level activity can be determined by:

- a judgment call that what the parties are doing does not distort or restrict competition and is therefore legal (something which is almost impossible to prove and which is therefore fraught with danger);
- being below certain prescribed thresholds of activity in terms of the market share of the businesses concerned (called *de minimis*);
- being expressly permitted by the competition legislation because there are specific rules in that market sector (block exemptions);
- the competition authorities examining the arrangement and declaring it permissible.

An anti-competitive arrangement is void. A third party adversely affected by such arrangement can sue the partners for damages and there may be penal sanctions (i.e. fines).

Joint ventures, because of their nature, will almost always raise competition law questions, and it is critical to have the arrangements scrutinized at an early stage so that these questions can be addressed. The worst-case scenario is where two direct competitors, each with a large market share, form a joint venture. At the other end of the spectrum, two small businesses working in different fields or at different levels of the supply chain (e.g. a software developer and a value-added reseller) are unlikely to face many general competition law issues. Price fixing is probably the biggest danger area for smaller businesses and this can arise indirectly as well as directly:

- partners dictate resale prices to the joint venture;
- partners provide a price list to the joint venture from which the joint venture may not deviate;

- partners set the joint venture's prices at a fixed margin over the suppliers' prices.

Specific advice should always be taken in this complex area.

APPENDIX: CHECKLIST FOR A JOINT VENTURE OPERATING AGREEMENT

This checklist sets out the main points which should be addressed irrespective of which business structure is adopted.

- Are the scope and nature of the joint venture clearly defined?
- What assets, resources (services and people) and finance will the joint venture need, both initially and over time? Which are to be provided by the partners and which from third parties?
- Are the partners providing trade mark licences or other IP to the joint venture?
- Are the partners trading with the joint venture (e.g. agency, distribution, licensing)? Are transfer pricing issues relevant?
- Are there any legal hurdles to overcome from the partners' perspective (e.g. is consent required from an investor to take shares in a joint venture)?
- Where is the joint venture to be physically located? Are the partners to provide premises (and associated services)? If so, on what terms?
- What computer hardware and software will the joint venture need? Where is it coming from and who will support it? Will additional licences be needed or can the software be operated on a bureau or application service provider basis from the partners? Will the systems have to interoperate with the partners' systems?
- Who are to be the professional advisers and suppliers (lawyers, auditors, tax advisers, insurers, etc.) to the joint venture?
- Does the joint venture need to be registered for VAT?
- Who handles the day-to-day personnel, management, payroll, etc. issues?
- Does the joint venture have appropriate Data Protection Act notification and can personal data be legitimately transferred between the partners and the joint venture?
- Are there any sector-specific regulatory issues?
- Are there any restrictions on the partners competing with each other or the joint venture? Have competition law aspects been considered? Do you need provisions preventing partners from poaching staff from the joint venture or each other?

- What is the nature and structure of the joint venture vehicle? What capital/income contributions are the partners to make?

- Should there be any restrictions on the sale of the partners' interest in the joint venture vehicle (e.g. shareholdings) to third parties or businesses within the partners' group?

- Who are the partners' representatives on the management team (e.g. appointed directors)?

- How are meetings of the partners (e.g. shareholders' meetings) and joint venture management (e.g. directors' meetings) to be convened and run? What decisions can be made at these meetings?

- What powers should be granted to the management team (e.g. are they allowed to raise bank borrowings without reference to the partners)?

- What is the procedure for introducing new partners or allowing existing partners to leave?

- What is the policy for accounting/distributing profits (e.g. a dividend policy)?

- What value (if any) is attributed to intangibles contributed by the joint venture partners?

- Is there a fixed or minimum term for the joint venture?

- What happens if there is a deadlock in decision-making between the partners?

- How does the management team get paid (if at all)? Are they entitled to expenses?

- Can a defaulting partner be forced to sell its interest? If so, at what price? How is that price calculated?

- What constitutes a default of the agreement? Breach of the main operating agreement? Breach of an ancillary agreement (e.g. a supply agreement)? Insolvency?

- What governing law is to cover the agreements (e.g. English)? Whose courts have jurisdiction? Is there a mechanism for dealing with disputes by escalation, arbitration or mediation?

Reproduced by permission of Moorcrofts

12 Resolving Disputes

SARA ELLACOTT

This chapter considers the various methods of dispute resolution available, their advantages and disadvantages together with a consideration of the relevant procedures associated with each method. Mediation is discussed after litigation and arbitration, but you should note that it is gaining popularity in the UK with both the courts and government agencies.

INTRODUCTION

Taking time to consider how to deal with potential disputes at the outset of a complex technology project can be viewed as being defeatist; parties are keen to work together and do not want to dwell on the potential difficulties they may face. The reality, however, is that during the life cycle of the majority of technology projects a variety of disputes will happen for a wide variety of reasons:

- business requirements change;
- delays mount up;
- complex terms give rise to various interpretations.

Despite the best intentions of the parties, careful planning and excellent working practices, problems can and do arise. Time is therefore well spent considering the various methods of dispute resolution available well before the need to utilize such methods arises.

DISPUTE RESOLUTION METHODS

At the outset of a dispute, unless your contract sets out exactly how it is to be handled, you are faced with a range of potential dispute resolution methods, the most common of which are:

- negotiation;
- escalation to senior management;
- expert determination;
- litigation;
- arbitration;
- competition bodies (for example, OFT, European Commission);
- mediation.

As there is no 'one size fits all' method of dispute resolution, your choice will ultimately depend on what you require out of the dispute resolution process, for example:

- Do you require damages/compensation for a particular breach of contract/misrepresentation?
- Is obtaining interim injunctive relief a necessity?
- Is an on-going relationship important?
- Is it important to maintain confidentiality as to the issues in dispute and the resulting settlement (if any)?

Depending on your needs, the different methods of dispute resolution will be more or less suitable. When deciding on any dispute resolution method there are a number of common factors which should be taken into account, these include:

- impartiality – is the adjudicator impartial and seen to be impartial?
- expertise – has the adjudicator the correct level of expertise to deal with the issues in dispute?
- speed – how long will it take the adjudicator to reach a decision?
- cost – how expensive will the process be?
- certainty – will the decision be binding and can it be appealed?
- confidentiality – will the decision/settlement be confidential?
- motivation – who, if anyone, has a vested interest in the dispute and its resolution?
- the business relationship – can the relationship continue after the dispute is resolved?
- ease of enforcement – can the decision be enforced domestically and/or abroad?

Each method of dispute resolution has its advantages and disadvantages. We will look at each method against the above factors before considering the relevant procedure associated with it.

Negotiation

Direct negotiation between the parties is one of the most successful (and popular) ways of resolving disputes. The following table shows how negotiation relates to the important factors in dispute resolution:

Impartiality	Not relevant (the parties are negotiating for their own benefit).
Expertise	Not particularly advantageous or relevant (although the people involved with the technology project will have first-hand knowledge of the issues in dispute and how they can be resolved).
Speed	Good: negotiations can be undertaken as quickly as the parties require (although they can drag on without any formal resolution taking place).

Cost	Good: the costs incurred will primarily be those of the individuals involved in the negotiations (additional costs may be incurred if the parties use internal or external legal advisors).
Certainty	Not good: the parties will come to a settlement only if they choose to do so.
Confidentiality	Good: such negotiations can be conducted on a 'without prejudice' and confidential basis. This encourages openness between the parties and ensures that the negotiations cannot be used in evidence if they break down and the parties end up using another form of dispute resolution. This is important, as the parties may be prepared to make concessions in their negotiating positions for the sake of reaching a compromise, which they would not be prepared to concede if they were litigating the dispute.
Motivation	Good: such negotiations usually involve those most heavily involved with the project on a day-to-day basis (the project manager, the IT director, the account manager, the commercial team, etc.). These parties are most closely aligned with the project and therefore have a vested interest in resolving the matters.
Business relationship	Good: such negotiations often allow for a positive on-going working relationship (in some cases, it can be stronger than the one that existed before the dispute). This is particularly important for those in technology projects, which often last for a number of years.
Enforcement	Not good: any settlement can only be enforced by one party suing the other for breach of contract (i.e. breach of the settlement terms). This can be time-consuming and expensive.

Escalation to senior management

Some technology contracts demand that the parties try and resolve disputes through senior management before resorting to external methods.

The advantages and disadvantages of this method of dispute resolution are very similar to those of negotiation. A particular advantage is in the area of motivation. Sometimes those at the 'coalface' of a large-scale technology project can become too emotionally involved to resolve a dispute – they allow their personal prejudices to prevent them seeing the advantages of a commercial resolution. Escalation to senior management can cut through such prejudices and allows for the 'bigger picture' to be considered and a commercial resolution found.

Expert determination

Expert determination is a popular method of dispute resolution in the construction industry and it is also well suited to the settlement of technology disputes. It is a procedure by which an independent third-party expert makes a decision on the dispute. The expert does not act as a judge or as an arbitrator. The following table shows how expert determination relates to the important factors in dispute resolution:

Impartiality	Good: as the parties have to agree on an expert they will only agree to someone they believe to be impartial.
Expertise	Good: the parties choose an individual who is an expert in the technology or project type (e.g. CRM, ERP) in dispute.
Speed	Good: the process can be set up as quickly as the parties can agree (subject to the expert's availability).
Cost	Good: in contrast to both litigation and arbitration, the process is inexpensive.
Certainty	Good: the result is contractually binding and thus difficult to appeal. This often brings finality to the dispute. The law on expert determination is, however, not conclusive and is developing. Moreover, there are no arrangements or laws which allow for the enforcement of an expert's decision abroad.
Confidentiality	Good: the procedure is confidential, which is clearly beneficial to a technology supplier, which would not want its customer base to become aware of any particular problems with its technology offering.
Motivation	Not a particularly relevant or overriding factor for this method of dispute resolution.
Business relationship	Good: expert determination may help to preserve a business relationship as it is slightly less adversarial than litigation or arbitration.
Enforcement	Good: failure to adhere to a decision will be a breach of contract. An expert's determination can thus be enforced by obtaining summary judgment and using general enforcement methods.

The procedure adopted for expert determination depends on the terms of the parties' contract (although they may decide to put a dispute to expert determination by later agreement). The 'terms of reference' set out how the expert is required to act and should include clear definitions of:

- the issues under dispute;
- the material the expert is expected to review;
- what the expert is allowed to consider (matters may arise from investigations which the parties to the dispute feel the expert is not equipped to deal with);
- the procedure and timescale to be followed;
- the nature of the submissions each party is allowed to make;
- what type of hearing is required;
- how the final decision is to be delivered (i.e. orally or in writing).

The expert is usually appointed from a recognized body. The parties may appoint a panel of experts rather than an individual, each person having been selected to provide a different type of expertise and perspective.

The parties may agree grounds upon which a decision may be challenged. If there is no express agreement, then common law inserts the following grounds as reason for appeal:

- fraud by the expert;
- failure by the expert to treat the two parties fairly or equally;

- a 'material departure' from the instructions, by the expert (any departure from the instructions that is more than trivial will be a 'material departure' irrespective of the consequences);

- a 'manifest error' by the expert (i.e. a blunder or omission capable of affecting the determination – it must have a significant consequential effect on the outcome of the determination; a minor mistake will not render the decision invalid, unless the parties have agreed that it will in their terms of reference);

- an error in an accountant's certificate which details the adjustment in value of a purchase price when that price is being determined by the expert.

Litigation

Litigation is the traditional method of resolving contractual disputes. The landscape of civil litigation changed with the introduction of the Civil Procedural Rules 1998 (CPR). The CPR places an emphasis on the front loading of legal costs, by the parties having to properly set out their claims at a much earlier stage in the proceedings than used to be the case. The following table shows how litigation relates to the important factors in dispute resolution:

Impartiality	Good: judges are impartial.
Expertise	Good: the technical expertise of judges has improved in recent years, particularly those in the Technology and Construction Court (TCC). Judges can also appoint experts to advise them on technical issues.
Speed	Not good: the courts are concerned with giving a decision (based on law) which is fair and objective. The speed of the decision-making process can therefore be secondary to obtaining a correct adjudication and the matter may go to appeal. The CPR allows for the courts to manage cases strictly and this should reduce the time scales of litigation. It is now possible to bring an action to trial within a year of the proceedings being commenced, particularly if the court orders a speedy trial (this is certainly no slower than most arbitrations). It is possible to make an application for urgent injunctive relief. This can often bring a matter to a very swift resolution; the party against whom the injunction is granted often looks for a commercial resolution at that time.
Cost	Not good: particularly if complex areas of IT law or technical matters have to be considered and expert evidence is required. The winning party does, however, generally have the ability to claim back a proportion of its costs from the losing party, which helps to reduce the financial burden.
Certainty	Good: litigation in the UK, and in most other jurisdictions, is governed by the rules of the relevant courts. The rules do allow for some flexibility but they are not as flexible as other forms of dispute resolution. Litigation has the advantage of finality (although the appeal process can lengthen the final outcome) and results in a binding judgment.

Confidentiality	Not good: most court papers and hearings are open to the public (the press can be admitted to the court room).
Motivation	Not a relevant or overriding factor.
Business relationship	Not good: as an adversarial process, litigation encourages tenacious contests, often bitterly fought by the parties.
Enforcement	Good: the binding judgment in a domestic technology dispute is enforceable through the courts. The position is less clear when one looks at international technology disputes: if the defendant is based outside the jurisdiction of the court and has no assets within that jurisdiction, the judgment may have little effect.

The procedure for litigation is:

i)   The party who believes its rights have been infringed (the 'Claimant') sends a 'letter before action' to the infringing party (the 'Defendant'). It is essential that the letter before action sets out the claim in sufficient detail to enable the defendant to fully understand the case against it. Thus the claimant generally must undertake a significant amount of preparation before sending this letter. When dealing with IT issues, this preparation can be particularly detailed and time-consuming.

ii) The defendant will usually respond in writing to the claimant's letter before action. At this stage, the parties may also attempt to negotiate a settlement on a 'without prejudice' basis (or explore alternative dispute resolution methods, particularly if required to do so by a contract between them).

iii) If the parties are unable to reach settlement, the claimant may elect to issue legal proceedings in the appropriate court (most likely the TCC). The claimant must serve upon the defendant a 'claim form' (a formal court form containing brief details of the claim) and 'particulars of claim' (a more detailed document setting out the claim and the remedies sought).

iv) The defendant must acknowledge service of the claim and may at that stage elect to admit the claim, or defend all or part of it. If intending to defend the claim, then the defendant must file with the court a 'defence' (a response to the claim, including the reasons why the defendant is not liable). A defendant who also has a claim against the claimant may file a 'counterclaim' (a document similar to the claimant's particulars of claim). If the defendant fails to acknowledge service of the claim or file a defence, the claimant may apply to the court for judgment in default of a defence.

v)   The court allocates the claim to the appropriate 'track' (small claims, fast-track or multi-track), depending upon the value and complexity of the claim. Technology disputes are dealt with by way of multi-track. Each party completes an allocation questionnaire providing details about the dispute to assist the court with allocation.

vi) The claimant may also choose to serve a 'reply' to the defendant's defence and a 'defence to counterclaim' if appropriate (if the claimant fails to defend a counterclaim, the defendant may apply for judgment in default). Unless there are exceptional circumstances, the claimant's reply and defence to the counterclaim brings an end to the process by which the parties set out their legal positions in writing. The remainder of the litigation process focuses upon the collection and exchange of each party's evidence.

vii) The court sets the timetable (or directions) for the further steps in the proceedings, including disclosure and inspection of the parties' documentary evidence, exchange of witness statements and expert reports, dates for any interim hearings (for example, the trial of a preliminary issue or a pre-trial review). The court is guided by information provided by the parties in their allocation questionnaires, which may include each party's preferred directions. The court may also order that the parties attend a hearing, known as a case management conference, to discuss directions. It is a particular feature of the CPR that the courts now take a very 'hands on' approach toward case management. It is fairly common for the directions to include a short stay of proceedings for the parties to attempt to reach settlement by alternative dispute resolution methods, such as mediation.

Following completion of the steps set out in the timetable for directions, the matter will go to trial. Trial may take the form of a single hearing, or the court has the option of trying a key preliminary issue on its own, on the basis that if this is decided in a certain party's favour it may end proceedings (or encourage an out-of-court settlement) and save the cost of a full hearing. After hearing the parties' cases at trial, the court gives its judgment and may grant leave to appeal.

There may also be a separate hearing to determine how legal costs are to be divided between the parties (generally the losing party pays the winner's costs, although the courts have a wide discretion to order costs on the most appropriate basis). If a party fails to comply with any order of the court, it may be necessary for the other party to go back to court to seek a further order for enforcement.

Arbitration

Arbitration is seen as the traditional alternative to litigation. It is a private and binding adjudicative process and was conceived as a way of providing a solution for commercial disputes in a practical/cost-effective way. The following table shows how arbitration relates to the important factors in dispute resolution:

Impartiality	Good: as the parties choose the arbitrator, it can be assumed that they are happy with the impartiality of the individual. In an international arbitration, it is common to have a tribunal of three arbitrators, with the chairman being neutral and each party appointing an arbitrator, who may well be of their nationality.
Expertise	Good: the appointed arbitrator will possess particular commercial or technical expertise. If necessary more than one arbitrator (one technical, one legal) can be appointed.
Speed	Good: arbitration offers some opportunities for innovation and for devising an appropriate cost-effective procedure for a particular dispute. The speed of domestic technology arbitrations may well rest on the development of such procedures. There are also opportunities for doing this in international technology arbitration, but the costs of such arbitrations are generally substantial.
Cost	Not good: a large-scale technology arbitration is likely to be as expensive, if not more so, than litigation. Arbitration is only cheaper if it disposes of a dispute more quickly and efficiently than court proceedings. Whether this is so depends on the co-operation of the parties to achieve that end. Since the arbitrator's engagement is a matter of contract, dates which are fixed will be kept by the tribunal. However, if the parties allow their disputes to spill over into the procedural conduct of the arbitration this may well nullify such cost benefits.
Certainty	Good: there is very little difference between litigation and arbitration in this respect; one of the main differences is that an arbitrator may not have to decide according to law. This does not mean that an arbitrator should disregard the rules of law but the parties can authorize the arbitrator to decide not strictly in accordance with the law.
Confidentiality	Good: only the parties to the dispute may attend the arbitration hearing and all documents prepared by both parties for the purpose of the arbitration are confidential and protected from disclosure in any subsequent proceedings. Although not true in all jurisdictions, non-statutory arbitration in the UK is private. This is a clear advantage as many arbitrations involve an investigation of material which is considered to be commercially sensitive, whether financially or because of the technology under consideration.
Motivation	Not a relevant or overriding factor.
Business relationship	Not good: arbitration is an adversarial process involving procedures which can be tenaciously utilized by lawyers. The outcome is often a breakdown in relationships.
Enforcement	Good: The Convention On The Recognition And Enforcement Of Foreign Arbitrary Awards 1958 (known as the 'New York Convention') provides for the awards from arbitration to be upheld internationally. The Convention has attracted near universal adherence (110 countries have signed up to it). Enforcement under the New York Convention is not always easy but it undoubtedly gives an arbitral award greater international effectiveness than a court judgment.

The framework for arbitration is governed by statute. Contracts often contain clauses which refer any dispute to arbitration. If such a clause exists, the parties must adhere to it rather than issuing proceedings in the courts. The parties to the contract select the arbitrator together on the basis of expertise in the field from which the dispute stems or on which the contract is based.

The arbitrator's conduct is governed by the ordinary rules of natural justice, evidence, and the civil burden of proof (the case must be proven 'on the balance of probabilities'). The parties are however at liberty to dispense with the ordinary rules of evidence and allow the arbitrator to carry out a more inquisitorial role.

If there is no governing arbitration clause, the parties may opt to engage in arbitration by agreement. In this instance, the parties meet and agree the terms of the arbitration agreement after the dispute has arisen. As is the case when an arbitration clause in a contract is being drafted, the parties are at liberty to determine the timescale, applicable law, procedure, and venue of the arbitration as well as the arbitrator they wish to use. In effect, the parties tailor the personnel, procedure and hearings to their particular needs.

During the arbitration proceedings, the arbitrator gives directions and may hold hearings in much the same way as a judge would in litigation proceedings. The arbitrator does this in accordance with the rules adopted by the parties, be they of their own invention or adopted from a particular institution's prescribed rules. The arbitrator may have to decide on the rules of the arbitration if the parties are unable to agree. The parties are able to refer issues to the courts if the arbitrator is guilty of any misconduct. The courts may also determine points of law and support the arbitrator by making various orders.

The arbitrator will hold a final hearing at which he will make an award to one of the parties. There is no requirement for the arbitrator to give reasons for the award he makes, however, if one of the parties asks for reasons and he refuses to give them, then the court (on application from the party concerned) may order him to do so. The award made is legally enforceable against the other party, however a party is allowed to appeal to the court against an award on a point of law.

Mediation

Mediation involves the appointment of an independent, qualified mediator (or mediators) to assist the parties in reaching an agreed settlement. A mediator does not usually have an adjudicative role in the mediation proceedings, nor is it the mediator's role (unless expressly asked to do so by the parties to the mediation) to pass judgment or to give an opinion on the merits of the parties' individual cases. Rather, the mediator's role is to facilitate the resolution of the dispute in question.

The use of mediation in the technology industry is on the increase, particularly as parties to a dispute now face increasing pressure from the courts to resolve their differences through alternative dispute resolution methods rather than court proceedings. The CPR states that the court must further the overriding objective by actively managing cases, including 'encouraging the parties to use an alternative dispute resolution procedure if the court considers that appropriate and facilitating the use of such procedure.' (Part 1.4(2)(e) of the CPR). There has been an increase in court-ordered mediations (in 2001–02, there was a 31% increase). Moreover, the government is encouraging the use of mediation in the public sector. Under the Lord Chancellor's Pledge, alternative dispute resolution methods should be considered and used in all suitable cases wherever the parties accept it. This covers government departments and agencies.

If a party in a technology dispute refuses an invitation to mediate, without a legitimate reason for such a refusal, it may risk being criticized by the courts should the dispute result in legal proceedings. That party could also face cost penalties regardless of the outcome of such legal proceedings should a court consider a refusal to mediate to constitute unreasonable conduct.

The following table shows how mediation relates to the important factors in dispute resolution:

Impartiality	Good: as the parties choose a mediator, they will be able to select a person who they regard as possessing impartiality.
Expertise	Not relevant: the mediator's expertise does not necessarily need to be legal or technical; it is more important that the mediator is well-trained and able to facilitate an open and constructive discussion. If necessary, the parties could appoint an additional, more technical, mediator.
Speed	Good: mediation ends when the parties reach a settlement, or when a party or mediator decides to terminate the process. Commonly, mediation does not last more than a day (much less time than arbitration or court proceedings). The time spent preparing for a mediation is also much less than the time spent preparing for litigation or arbitration.
Cost	Good: the costs are a fraction of those which would be incurred were legal proceedings to be initiated. Moreover, the significant costs orders and damages awards that may be awarded in court proceedings can be avoided.
Certainty	Moderate: if successful, mediation results in the resolution by an agreement of the parties. It may not be a 'correct' legal decision, but resolution will in general be 'fair' because it will be consented to by both parties.
Confidentiality	Good: mediation is a strictly confidential process. All representations made during this process (whether written or oral) are also 'without prejudice' and therefore any documentation produced for the purposes of the mediation and admissions made during it cannot, in most cases, be relied upon as evidence by the parties in court proceedings should the mediation prove unsuccessful.
Motivation	Good: parties who agree to mediate are usually committed to reaching a commercially acceptable resolution, particularly if an on-going business relationship is a possibility.
Business relationship	Good: as the mediation process is significantly closer to business negotiations than to adversarial courtroom procedures, business relationships can better be preserved.

Enforcement	Not good: the process of mediation is non-binding and the parties cannot be forced to settle their dispute unless a consensus to do so is reached. If a settlement is agreed, it only becomes binding upon the parties once the terms have been recorded in a settlement agreement and the agreement is executed by all parties concerned. If a party refuses to carry out the settlement, it is necessary to commence an action on the settlement agreement, to obtain judgment and then to seek execution of the judgment. Experience, however, suggests that parties who have mediated a settlement of their dispute tend to voluntarily carry out the terms of settlement and that a formal enforcement procedure is rarely necessary.

The parties are expected to agree upon a choice of mediator. The choice of mediator will invariably be determined by the nature of the dispute, and the mediator may be a lawyer, an accountant or a technical expert. In the IT industry, a legally-qualified mediator with knowledge of the industry, or possibly a technically-qualified expert, would be preferable. A venue for the mediation also needs to be agreed upon. This is usually a venue independent of the parties.

The process usually follows this format:

i)   The parties prepare written case summaries that are exchanged with each other and provided to the mediator in advance of the mediation. This allows the mediator to understand the issues in dispute and the parties' respective positions. The case summaries should highlight any facts/issues which have been agreed by the parties as well as those which remain in dispute. These summaries are usually supported by an agreed bundle of relevant documentation to which the parties can refer in their summaries. This is usually made up of contracts, correspondence, notes of meetings, relevant technical papers, etc. The mediation takes place shortly after the exchange of case summaries and copy documentation.

ii) The mediation commences with a joint session attended by all the parties (and their legal representatives) and the mediator, at which the parties are invited to give a short presentation of their positions in relation to the dispute.

iii) The parties retire to separate rooms and a series of what are termed 'caucus' sessions commence. The sessions involve the mediator visiting each of the parties to discuss and explore their respective legal positions. The mediator will use these caucus sessions to establish if there is any middle ground between the parties which may form the basis of a negotiated settlement.

iv) The mediator may call the parties back for further open sessions to discuss any progress that has been made or issues that have been raised.

v)   If the parties are successful in establishing a commercial resolution to the dispute the mediator will expect them to sign up to written terms of settlement prior to the close of the mediation. Most mediation organizations insist upon the parties having personnel with the appropriate authority to settle the dispute. Mediators are particularly keen on any agreement reached being drawn up and signed by the parties on the day of the mediation, as this avoids the parties subsequently disputing the terms of any agreement reached.

CONCLUSION

There is no 'right answer' when choosing a dispute resolution process. Each dispute resolution method has advantages and disadvantages which will play a part in the decision-making process.

Mediation is gaining popularity in the UK (with both the courts and government agencies) as a commercial and cost-effective way of resolving disputes. This applies equally to disputes in the technology arena. A refusal to consider this dispute resolution method could have heavy cost implications.

Index

acceptance criteria, for consultants
59–60
acceptance testing
definition xiv
in hardware purchase contracts 5
procedure for 13, 18
in software development contracts
9
in systems procurement contracts
18
access requests by data subjects *see*
data subjects
access to system, policy on staff usage
47–48
agencies, finding consultants through
51–52
agency agreements, as joint ventures
130
alternative dispute resolution (ADR),
definition xiv
application service provider (ASP),
definition xiv, 85
arbitration, as dispute resolution
method 145–147
arbitrator 146–147
asset register 92
asset transfer 91–92

backup of data
copies of software 63
data protection issues 106
specimen policy on 48–49
benchmarking 90–91
British Computer Society
contact details ii
disciplinary procedure 57
finding consultants through 53–54
professional advice register 53–54
Worklink service 53
Brussels Convention 120
business
email
confidentiality of 48
disclaimers on 40, 42–43
information disclosure in 42–43
record-keeping 48
security in 48
specimen policy on 48
letters, information disclosure in
42–43
Business Names Act 1985, information
disclosure requirements 43
business process outsourcing (BPO),
definition xiv, 85
business to business contracts,
jurisdiction in 120

cancellation rights, under Distance
Selling Directive 118–119
change control
clause in contract 18–19
definition xiv
Civil Procedure Rules 1998 (CPR)
definition xiv
dispute resolution, role in 143, 145
mediation, encouragement of 147
claimant, definition xiv
Code of Advertising Practice 105
Community designs 75
Companies Act 1985, information
disclosure requirements 43
Competition Act 1998 135
competition bodies, role in dispute
resolution 139
competition law
definition xiv
joint ventures and 135–137
Computer Misuse Act 1990 42
computer usage policies
action plan on 43
backup of data 48–49
confidentiality 48
data protection 48
drawing up 41
generally 38–43
misuse 49
password protection 48
record-keeping 48
security of data 48
specimen 46–49
confidential information, protection of
72–73
confidentiality
in business emails 48
in consultancy services contracts 5
in IT contracts 12
in source code escrow agreements
82
consequential loss, liability for 22–235
consultancy services, contracts for
confidentiality in 5
copyright in 4–5
deliverables in 4
generally 4–5
insurance in 5
key personnel in 5
payment arrangements in 4
termination rights 5
consultants
acceptance criteria for 59–60
assessing suitability of 54–55, 56
disputes with 57
finding *see* sources of
handovers from 57

instructing 50–60
pricing structures 55–56
relationship with 57
selecting 54–55, 56
sources of
academic sources 53
agencies 51–53
British Computer Society 53–54
internet, the 54
management consultancies 52–53
personal recommendation 55
systems integrators 52
Terms of Reference document
acceptance criteria, on 59–60
assumptions in 58–59
deliverables, on 59
importance of 56, 57–58
reporting requirements 59
resources, on 59
scope of 58
template for 58–60
timescale for 56
consumer, definition 113
consumer contracts, jurisdiction in
120
Consumer Protection (Distance
Selling) Regulations 2000
cancellation rights 118–119
information requirements 115–116
non-compliance, consequences of
121–122
Stop Now Orders 121–122
contra proferentem rule 24
contracts
boilerplate terms 1–2
business to business, jurisdiction in
120
consultancy services, for 4–5
consumer, jurisdiction in 120
contra proferentem rule 24
electronic *see* ecommerce
entire agreement clause 2
exclusion clauses 21–28
implied terms 14–15
legal structure 116–117
force majeure clause xv, 2
formation of 12–13, 116–118
governing law and jurisdiction
clause 2
hardware maintenance, for 6–7
hardware purchase, for 5–6
in IT *see* IT contracts
service level agreements (SLAs)
10–11
software development, for 9–10
software licences, for 7
software maintenance, for 7– 9

standard, dangers of 15–16
Convention on the Recognition and
	Enforcement of Foreign
	Arbitrary Awards 1958 (New
	York Convention) 146
cookies
	definition xiv
	regulation of use 105
copyright
	in consultancy services contracts
		4–5, 20
	creation of 71
	databases, in 71
	definition xiv, 70
	in developed software 10, 20, 77
	duration of 70–71
	the internet and 70
	manuals, in 71
	moral rights and 71
	registration of 71
	software, in 71
	website contents 6–67, 71
country of origin principle 119–120
customer computer system
		procedures, policy on staff
		usage 47
customer relationship management
	(CRM), definition xiv

data controller
	definition xv, 96
	notification procedure for 99–100,
		110
data protection
	backup tapes 106
	and business emails 40, 48
	consent to processing 102–103
	data subject rights *see* data subjects
	enforcement 110–111
	exemption from requirements
		notification 98–99, 110
		subject access provisions 110
		subject information provisions
			110
	list brokers, obtaining information
		from 102
	marketing, opting out of 104–105
	notification with Information
		Commissioner
		changes to 100
		exemption from requirements
			98–99, 110
		liable parties 98–99
		procedure 99–100
		renewal of 100
		templates for 100
	penalties 110–111
	personal data
		definition of 96–97
		security of
			British Standard on 107
			procedures for 99–100, 106–107
			'proportionality' in 107
		sensitive *see* sensitive personal
			data, below
		transfer to other countries
			107–108
	principles

accurate 103–104
	adequate, relevant and not
		excessive 103
	fair and lawful processing
		101–102
	generally 101–108
	not kept longer than necessary
		105–106
	not transferred to countries
		without adequate protection
		107–108
	processed in accordance with data
		subject's rights 106
	processing for limited purposes
		102
	secure 106–107
'processing'
	consent to 102–103
	definition of 101
	fair and lawful 101–102
	in accordance with subject's rights
		106
	limited purposes, for 102
	third parties, by 107
	scope 96–97
	security of personal data
		British Standard on 107
		procedures 99–100, 106–107
		'proportionality' in 107
	sensitive personal data
		consent to processing of 102, 103
		definition xvii, 97–98
	subject access provisions *see* data
		subjects
	subject information provisions *see*
		data subjects
	terminology 95–96
Data Protection Act 1998
	data controller, definition of xv, 96
	Enforcement Notices 110–111
	exemptions
		notification, from 98–99, 110
		subject access provisions, from
			110
		subject information provisions,
			from 110
	marketing, right to opt out of
		104–105
	notification
		exemption from requirements
			98–99, 110
		procedure 99–100
		'personal data' under 96–97,
			99–100, 106–108, 108–108
	principles of data protection, on
		101
	scope 96–97
	'sensitive personal data' under xvii,
		97–98, 102, 103
	subject access provisions *see* data
		subjects
	subject information provisions *see*
		data subjects
	terminology 95–96
Data Protection Registrar *see*
	Information Commissioner
data subjects
	access requests

complying with 109–110
		definition xvii
		exemptions from 110
		time limit for 110
	consent to processing 102–103
		definition xv
	information provisions
		complying with 101
		exemptions from 110
	marketing, opting out of 104–105
	provision of details to 101
	rights of
		access requests 109–110
		information on processor,
			receiving 109, 110
		marketing, opting out of 104–105
		processing in accordance with
			106
database rights xiv, 65–66, 76
databases
	copyright in 71
	and intellectual property rights
		65–66, 71
	licences to use 65
	protecting own rights in 65–66
	rights in *see* database rights
decompilation of software 64
decompiler, definition xv
defendant, definition xv
deliverables
	consultant's Terms of Reference
		document on 59
	defining
		in consultancy services contracts
			4
		in service level agreements 10
	description, implied contractual term
		as to 14–15
design rights
	Community designs 75
	definition xv
	UK registered designs 74
	UK unregistered design right 74–75
design risk 87
direct marketing, data subjects' right
	to opt out of 104–105
Direct Marketing Association 104–105
Disability Discrimination Act 1995 45
disclaimers, on business emails 40,
	42–43
disks, policy on staff usage 46
display screen equipment (DSE)
	definition xv
	employers' duties regarding 44–45
	legislation on *see* DSE Regulations
dispute avoidance, in domain name
	registration 68
dispute resolution (DR); *see* also
		alternative dispute resolution
		(ADR)
	arbitration 145–147
	competition bodies, through 140
	in consultancy contracts 57
	definition xv
	escalation to senior management
		141
	expert determination 141–143
	litigation 143–145

mediation 147–150
methods 139–150
negotiation 140–141
'distance contracts', information
    requirements 114–157
distance selling, definition xv
Distance Selling Directive
    cancellation rights 118
    information requirements 114,
        115–116
    performance time limits 118
Distance Selling Regulations *see*
    Consumer Protection (Distance
    Selling) Regulations 2000
distribution agreements, as joint
    ventures 130
domain names
    'cyber-squatters' 67
    definition xv
    dispute avoidance 68
    and intellectual property rights
        67–68
    problems with 67
    registration of 67–68
    and trade marks 67
DSE Regulations 44–45
due diligence
    in asset transfer 92
    definition xv
    investigations 36–37
    in IT 35–37
    in selecting an IT consultant 54

ecommerce
    authorization schemes 113–114
    cancellation rights 118–119
    Consumer Protection (Distance
        Selling) Regulations 2000
        115–116
    consumer rights enforcement in
        121
    contract formation 116–118
    country of origin principle 119–120
    generally 112–124
    information requirements
        consolidated checklist 124
        Consumer Protection (Distance
        Selling) Regulations 2000
        115–116
        Distance Selling Directive 114,
        115–116
        Electronic Commerce Directive
        114–115, 117–118
        Electronic Commerce (EC
        Directive) Regulations 2002
        114–115, 117–118
        enforcement of duties 121–122
        information sources 123
        jurisdiction in 119–120
        marketing communications
        120–121
        performance time limits 118
        spam, restrictions on sending 121
        Stop Now Orders 121–122
        terminology 113
        VAT issues 122–123
Economic and Monetary Union
    (EMU), definition xv

Electronic Commerce Directive
    authorization schemes 113–114
    contract formation by electronic
        means 117
    information requirements 114–115,
        117–118
    information society service
        providers, operating rules for
        119–120
    marketing communications
        120–121
Electronic Commerce (EC Directive)
    Regulations 2002
    information requirements 114–115,
        117–118
    information society service
        providers
    enforcement action against 121–122
    operating rules for 119–120
    marketing communications
        120–121
    non-compliance, consequences of
        121–122
    spam, rules on sending 121
    Stop Now Orders 121–122
electronic contracts *see* ecommerce
Electronic Money Institutions
    Directive 112
Electronic Signatures Directive 112
email
    business
        confidentiality in 48
        data protection and 48
        disclaimers on 40, 42–43
        password protection in 48
        record-keeping in 48
        security in 48
        specimen policy on 48
    confidentiality 48
    data protection and 48
    disclaimers, in business 40, 42–43
    employees' misuse of, consequences
        for employers 38, 39
    monitoring by employers 39–41,
        47–48
    password protection 48
    private, employees'
        monitoring by employers 39–41
        specimen restriction on 47–48
        usage policies 41
    problems with 38–39
    security in 48
    storage, problems caused by 39
    unsolicited *see* spam
    usage policies
        action plan on 43
        establishing 41–42
        monitoring 39–41
        private, employees' 39–41, 47–48
        specimen 47–48
Email Preference Service 104
employees
    customer systems usage 47
    internet usage
        action plan on 43
        inappropriate material 47
        monitoring by employers 39–41
        policy considerations 41

    specimen restriction on 47–49
    licensed software usage 47
    misuse of computer systems,
        consequences for employers
        38, 39
    private email
        monitoring by employers 39–41,
        47–48
        specimen restriction on 47–48
        usage policies 41
    screen users' rights 44–45
employers
    consequences of staff misuse of
        computers 38, 39
    monitoring of staff communications
        39–41, 41–42, 47–48, 49
    screen users, duties towards 44–45
employment problems, avoiding
    38–49
Enforcement Notices, under Data
    Protection Act 1998 110–111
Enterprise Resource Planning (ERP),
    definition xv
entire agreement clause 2
escalation clauses
    as dispute resolution method 141
    in service level agreements 12
escrow
    advantages for software owners 83
    agents 81–83
    agreements, elements of 81–82
    definition xv, 76
    importance for software users 76–77
    source code, for *see* source code
        escrow
    user's duties 82
European Economic Area (EEA),
    definition xv
European economic interest grouping
    (EEIG), legal liability of
    134–135
exclusion clauses in contracts
    contra proferentem rule 24
    enforcement of 23–25
    forms of 21–23
    'reasonableness' test
        application in practice 26–28
        satisfying 24–25
expert determination, as dispute
    resolution method 141–143
eye tests for screen users 45

facilities management (FM) contract,
    definition xv, 85
Fax Preference Service 104
fitness for purpose of goods, implied
    term as to 15
force majeure
    as boilerplate contractual term 2
    definition xv
framing
    definition xv
    in trade mark infringement 69–70

goodwill, protection of *see* passing off

hacking 42
hardware

authorized sales 62
and intellectual property rights
61–63
maintenance *see* hardware
maintenance
purchase *see* hardware purchase
repairs 63
special conditions of sale 62–63
hardware maintenance
contracts for
generally 6–7
important terms 5–6
payment arrangements 6
termination rights 19
types 6
hardware purchase, contracts for 5–6
health and safety
action plan on 45–46
avoiding claims 43–46
DSE Regulations 44–45
law on 44
screen quality 44–45
Health and Safety at Work etc. Act
1974 45
Health and Safety (Display Screen
Equipment) Regulations 1992
see DSE Regulations
home state regulation 119

implementation of new systems *see*
system implementations
implied terms of contracts 14–15
Information Commissioner
definition xvi
enforcement role 110–111
notification with *see* data protection
title 95
information society service providers
data protection considerations for
98–100
definition 113
enforcement action against 121–122
operating rules 119–120
information society services, definition
113
information technology (IT)
consultants *see* consultants
contracts in *see* IT contracts
definition xvi
due diligence in 35–37
functions commonly outsourced 86
in mergers and acquisitions 35
Institute of Management Consultancy
(IMC) 52, 57
insurance, in consultancy services
contracts 5
intellectual property
definition 61
rights in *see* intellectual property
rights (IPRs)
intellectual property law, for computer
users 61–75
intellectual property rights (IPRs)
databases and 65–66
definition xvi, 61
domain names and 68–68
guide to 70–75
hardware and 61–63

infringement on the web 69
in joint ventures 128–129
software and 63–65
in systems procurement contracts
20–21
terminology 70–75
websites and 66–67, 68–71
interception of communications, by
employers *see* monitoring, by
employers
interface, definition xvi
internet, the
and copyright 70
finding consultants through 54
staff usage
action plan on 43
inappropriate material 47
monitoring by employers 39–41
policy considerations 41
specimen restriction on 47–49
and trade marks 68–70
IT consultants *see* consultants
IT contracts
boilerplate terms 1–2
confidentiality 12
deliverables, defining 4
lawyer, choice of 2
letter of intent 3
main points of 1–2, 12–13
standard terms *see* boilerplate terms,
above; suppliers, below
suppliers
suitability, assessing 2–3
terms proposed by 3, 57–16
terms
standard *see* boilerplate terms,
above; suppliers' proposed,
below
suppliers' proposed 5
types of, *see* consultancy services;
hardware maintenance;
hardware purchase; service
level agreements (SLAs);
software development; software
licences; software maintenance

joint ventures
agency model in 130
agreement, terms of 127
'bolt on' terms 130–131
business plans for 127–128
Case Study on 126
competition law and 135–137
definition of xvi, 125
distribution model in 130
establishing 126–129
exit arrangements 129
heads of agreement 127
intellectual property ownership
128–129
and IT projects 125–126
in licensing deals 130
management 128
non-disclosure agreements 126–127
operating agreement 135, 137–138
structures 129–135
jurisdiction, in contracts 119–120

key performance indicators (KPIs) 88

lawyer, choice of 2
legal persons 132
letter of intent 3
liability
legal 132–133, 134–135
limited 132–133
licences *see* databases; software
licences
licensed software, policy on staff usage
46
licensing deals, joint venture
arrangements in 130
limited companies 132–134
limited liability 132–134
limited liability corporations 134
limited liability partnerships (LLPs)
133–134
limited partnerships 132
linking
definition xvi
trade mark infringement caused by
69–70
list brokers, obtaining information
from 102
litigation
as dispute resolution method
143–145
procedure 143, 144–145

management, dispute resolution
through 141
management consultancies, finding
consultants through 52–53
Management Consultancies
Association (MCA) 52–53, 57
Management of Health and Safety at
Work Regulations 1999 44
manuals, copyright in 71
market testing 90–91
marketing, data subjects' right to opt
out of 104–105
marketing communications, in
ecommerce 120–121
Mailing Preference Service 105
mediation, as dispute resolution
method 147–150
mergers and acquisitions, IT in 35
metatags
definition xvi
use in trade mark infringement 70
migration arrangements, in service
level agreements 11
misuse of computer systems
consequences for employers 38, 39
examples 49
specimen policy on 49
monitoring, by employers
emails 39–41, 48, 49
internet use 41–42, 47–48, 49
telecommunications 39, 40, 49
website access 41–42
moral right
copyright, relationship with 71
definition xvi

negotiation

as dispute resolution method
140–141
in systems procurement contracts
14
networks, policy on staff usage 46
non-disclosure agreement (NDA)
definition xvi
use in joint ventures 126–127
notification with Information
Commissioner *see* data
protection

object code, definition xvi
original equipment manufacturer
(OEM), definition xvi
output specification 86
outputs and inputs, distinguishing
86–87
outsourcing
asset transfer 91–92
definition xvi, 85
design risk 87
exit arrangements 93
key elements 85
key performance indicators (KPIs)
88
life cycle of 91–93
offshore 94
performance indicators (PIs) 88
performance points 88
pricing and payment mechanisms
89–91
ratchet mechanisms 88–89
service delivery phase 93
service description drafting 86
service level agreement 87–89
specification 86
transition of services 92–93

partnership
agreements 132
characteristics of 132, 134
disclosure of information on letters
43
legal definition of 131
limited 132
limited liability 133–134
Partnership Act 1890 132
passing off
definition xvi
introduction 73–74
password protection, in business
email 48
patents
application procedure 72
definition xvi
duration of 72
scope of 71–72
software, of 72
payment arrangements
in consultancy services contracts 4
in hardware maintenance contracts
6
in outsourcing contracts 89–91
in software development contracts
9
in software maintenance contracts
9

in systems procurement contracts
19–20
performance indicators (PIs) 88
performance points 88
personal data *see* data protection
pricing structures
for IT consultants 55–56
in outsourcing contracts 89–91
Privacy and Electronic
Communications (EC Directive)
Regulations 2003
cookies, regulation of use 105
unsolicited email, restrictions on
sending 105, 121
unsolicited text messages,
restrictions on sending 105
problem management, in systems
procurement contracts 21–24
processing of data *see* data protection
professional advice register 53–54
project open book accounting (POBA)
90
'proportionality', in personal data
security 107

quality of goods, implied contractual
term as to 15
quiet possession of goods, implied
contractual term as to 14

rapid application development (RAD),
definition xvi
ratchet mechanisms 88–89
reasonable care and skill, implied
contractual term as to 15
'reasonableness' test in exclusion
clauses
application in practice 26–28
satisfying 24–25
recording business dealings 48
Regulation of Investigatory Powers Act
2000 39, 40
repetitive strain injury (RSI)
action plan on reducing 45–46
definition xvii
level of claims 44
reseller agreement 130
retention of title, in hardware supply
contracts 20
royalty deals, joint venture
arrangements in 130

scoping new systems projects 32–33
screen users, employers' duties
towards 44–45
screens *see* display screen equipment
(DSE)
security
in business emails 48, 49
of personal data 99–100, 106–107
sensitive personal data *see* data
protection
service description drafting 86
service level agreements (SLAs)
breach of 11
compensation arrangements 11
contracts for 10–11
definition xvii

deliverables 10
elements of 89
escalation clauses 11
form of 11
main terms 10–11
migration arrangements 13
outsourcing, for 87–89
termination rights 11
service provider, definition 113
service recipient, definition 113
software
adapting 63, 64
backup copies 63
copying 63, 64
copyright in 71
decompilation 64
development *see* software
development
and intellectual property rights
63–65
licences *see* software licences
maintenance *see* software
maintenance
patenting of 72
staff usage of licensed 46
supply contracts, special
considerations in 25
software development
contracts for
generally 9–10
payment arrangements 9
special considerations in 25
termination rights 19
copyright in product 10
source code escrow and 10
supplier's warranty in 10
software houses *see* systems
integrators
software licences
agreements 7
contracts for 7
non-compliance with 65
permitted uses under 26, 46
requirements for 63
restrictions imposed by 25
scope of 63, 64
and staff usage 46
transferring 64
software maintenance, contracts for
charging arrangements 8–9
common terms 8
exclusions from 8
generally 7–9
payment arrangements 9
scope of services 8
termination rights 9
sole traders, disclosure of information
on letters 43
source code
complexity of 79
conversion to executable code 76
definition xvii, 76
deposit agreements *see* source code
escrow
escrow for *see* source code escrow
security of, reasons for 77
storage issues 83
source code escrow

advantages for software owners 83
agents 81–83
agreements, elements of 81–82
generally 76–84
items to be lodged 80–81
need for 77–79
and proof of ownership of software
83
providing for in IT contracts 13
release events 79, 81
reasons for using 77–79
and software development 10
technical considerations 79
verification 80
spam
definition xvii
legal restrictions on sending 105,
121
specification
definition xvii
in implementation of new systems
31–32
in systems procurement contracts
16–17
staff transfers, TUPE and 93–94
staff usage of computers *see*
employees
standard contracts, dangers of 15–16
statement of requirements 86
Stop Now Orders 121–122
Structured Systems Analysis and
Design Method (SSADM),
definition xvii
subject access provisions *see* data
subjects
subject information provisions *see*
data subjects
suppliers
suitability of, assessing 2–3, 31
terms proposed by 3, 15–16
warranties given by
in software development
contracts 10
in systems procurement contracts
21
system access, policy on staff usage
47–48
system implementations
Case Study 34
planning, role of 33–34
realizing benefits 35
scoping 32–33
setting expectations in 30–31
specification, role of 31–32
system requirements, specifying
31–32
systems integration (SI), definition
xvii
systems integrators (SIs), finding
consultants through 52
systems procurement
contracts for *see* systems

procurement contracts
definition xvii
systems procurement contracts
acceptance testing 18
breach of, remedies for 21
change control 18–19
client obligations 16, 18
consequential loss liability in 22–23
delivery arrangements 17
exclusion clauses in
contra proferentem rule 24
enforcement of 23–25
forms of 21–23
'reasonableness' test 24–25, 26–28
implied terms of 14–15
intellectual property rights 20–21
liquidated damages in 21
mechanics of 16–19
negotiation process 14–15
payment arrangements 19–20
pricing structures 19
principal obligations 16
problem management in 21–24
remedies, contractual, in 21
specification 16–17
standard contracts, dangers of
15–16
supplier warranties 21
termination rights 19
terms implied by law 14–15
timetable in 17

technical solution 86
Technology and Construction Court
(TCC)
definition xvii
dispute resolution, role in 143, 144
Telecommunications (Data Protection
and Privacy) Regulations 1999
104
Telecommunications (Lawful Business
Practice) (Interception of
Communications) Regulations
2000 40
Telephone Preference Service 104
termination rights
in consultancy services contracts 19
in hardware maintenance contracts
19
in outsourcing contracts 93
in software development contracts
19
in systems procurement contracts
19
terms, contractual
boilerplate 1–2
implied by law 14–15
of IT contracts *see* IT contracts
of joint ventures 127
standard *see* boilerplate terms,
above; suppliers' proposed,
below

suppliers' proposed 3, 15–16
Terms of Reference document, for
consultants *see* consultants
title to goods
implied term as to 14
retention of, in hardware supply
contracts 20
trade marks
application procedure 73
definition xvii
domain names and 67
infringement of 68–70, 73
the internet and 68–70
linking, infringement caused by
69–70
metatags, infringement caused by
70
registrability 73
websites, signs used on 66
Transfer of Undertakings (Protection
of Employment) Regulations
1981 (TUPE)
definition xvii
and staff transfers 93–94

unsolicited communications,
restrictions on sending
email *see* spam
text messages 105
usage policies
computers 38–43, 48–49
email 38–43, 47–48
specimen 46–49

value added tax
definition xvii
in ecommerce 122–123
verification, definition xvii
viruses, policy on staff action against
46–47

warranties
clients', as to IPRs 20–21
suppliers'
in software development
contracts 10
in systems procurement contracts
21
websites
copyright in 66–67, 71
intellectual property rights in
generally 66–67
infringement of 67, 68–70
linking in, trade mark infringement
caused by 69–70
metatags, trade mark infringement
caused by 70
monitoring staff access, by
employers 41–42
ownership of 66
protection of rights in 66–67
Worklink service 53